Nzingha,
you are a beautiful
Queen of God. I love your
energy and your spirit for your
gifts bless all who know you.
Love you,
Lashana W.

THE STRANGER WITHIN

One Woman's Journey to Self-Love

D0813964

Lashana N Williams

ISBN: 0996762604
ISBN 13: 9780996762601

TABLE OF CONTENTS

This book is dedicated to anyone who battles with the demon of self-hate.
I hope through my journey, you will be victorious, too.

INTRODUCTION

L ow self-esteem is assumed to only affect people with a troubled childhood, a physical defect or mental disorder. It is true people who suffer from one or all of these conditions may be more susceptible to low self-esteem (diminished self-love), but they are not the only ones who find themselves a victim to self-hatred or as I like to call it, the "demon of self-hate." The demon of self-hate doesn't discriminate. It attacks all people from all walks of life and can take on many forms. You would be astonished to learn of who and how many people battle with the demon of self-hate every day of their lives.

It may have come as a surprise when Halle Berry admitted to the world that she suffers from low self-esteem. It's hard to believe that a beautiful, successful woman like Halle Berry would ever see herself as unattractive and unworthy of being loved. However, in her own words Halle Berry stated, "I think I've spent my adult life dealing with the sense of low self-esteem that sort of implanted in me, somehow I felt not worthy. Before I'm Halle Berry I'm little Halle…a little girl growing in this environment that damaged me…I've spent my adult life trying to really heal from that." (Vogue, September 2010)

Halle Berry, although a superstar in the eyes of society, isn't any different from you or me. She eats, breathes and sleeps, just like we do. But when people look at her, they see beauty, money and fame. Many would say, "She's got it made." If only people looked past her exterior. It is there where she hurts, where she cries, and where her internal struggle takes place. Like myself, she probably faked it until she made it; putting on a mask every day in hope that one day she would be able to truly love herself.

Halle Berry isn't the only celebrity who has openly admitted to suffering from low self-esteem. In an interview about her Monster Ball Tour at Madison Square Garden, Lady Gaga stated, "I just feel like a loser still. It's crazy because we're at The Garden, but I still sometimes feel like a loser kid in high-school… I have to pick myself up and tell myself I am a superstar every morning to get through the day."

Like Lady Gaga, I remember feeling out of place in school. In high school, people were known for something. There were the jocks, the nerds, the bad boys/girls, the fashionistas, the "cool" kids etc. I didn't belong in any of these groups, and since I wasn't confident enough to just be me, I became the person I thought people wanted me to be. In my eyes I was no one...I hated myself. If only I could have been someone else...if only I could have been anyone else but me.

WHY I WROTE THIS BOOK

Although its mere existence results in the same unfortunate emotional state– an absence of self-love – the way in which the demon of self-hate invades one's life may vary. Some of us may suffer from low self-image, while others may experience low self-confidence or self-worth. Upon reading further, you'll see that your girl (me) was attacked in all three areas. Man, the demon of self-hate had it in for me!

Despite its approach, the only way to truly obtain self-love – a healthy self-esteem – is to evict the demon of self-hate from your mind, body, and spirit, thus destroying the power and the hold it has over your life. The demon of self-hate isn't a stranger to destroying lives. It sneaks in like a thief in the night. First, it obtains your trust and then before you know it, the demon is attacking your mind. Have you ever wondered how the positive perception you had of yourself as a toddler (you were invincible, cute as a button, and not afraid of saying whatever came to mind) transformed into negative thoughts, doubts and self-loathing?

There are hundreds of self-help books that do a good job of summarizing the topic how to overcome low self-esteem or how to rebuild self-love, providing helpful techniques for the reader to overcome their battle in 7 to 21 easy steps. Huh, if only it was that easy. After reading over fifty self-help books, I'm now a self-proclaimed doctor on the topic. My reading only increased my knowledge, but unfortunately, didn't help me get any closer to overcoming my own internal battle.

Even some talk shows have tried to provide viewers with a foolproof way to overcome low self-esteem within a 30-minute or an hour segment. For those of us who have battled or are currently battling this demon, thirty minutes isn't enough to adequately describe the thoughts, feelings, emotions and pain one may experience on a daily basis. It definitely isn't enough time to provide a cure.

I question why this very important topic tends to be addressed as if it's this cute little problem that could easily be summarized and fixed within 200 pages of a book or a 30-minute segment of a talk show. Understanding the importance of this topic and realizing that a great number of people battle with some form of internal conflict – low self-image, self-worth or self-confidence – I wrote this book in hope that sharing my journey to self-love will help you or someone you know to one day be victorious over the demon of self-hate.

HOW TO READ THIS BOOK

In this book, I invite you to accompany me on my journey as I uncover the events and people who contributed to my low self-esteem. Along my journey, I will share lessons learned and words of encouragement, hoping that together, we will discover ways for you or someone you know to be victorious in your own internal battle.

This journey has helped me learn, understand, and accept the woman I am today. Although necessary, my exploration forced me to relive events that were once buried in my subconscious. These events, whether good or bad, have shaped the woman I am today, but the memories are a reminder of the hurt and pain I endured along the way.

It's important for you as the reader, and as my friend along this journey, to know that I'm telling my truth, and each event is told through my eyes based on my perception, feelings and emotions at that time. I also took the liberty of changing the names of those highlighted in the book. The names of the people are not important. While reading each chapter, the focus should be on the experiences that led to the unwelcomed presence of the demon of self-hate and the steps I took to rebuild my self-esteem.

I hope that after reading the first page of this book, we have become friends, and as such, I ask that you join me as I laugh, cry, and sometimes curse while I replay the events that caused me to dislike myself. I share with you some of the most vulnerable times in my life, hoping that my story may help you or someone you know in successfully overcoming the damaging effects of the demon of self-hate.

My journey is broken up into three parts...

PART I: SELF-IMAGE - Due to the actions and words of others, I believed I was incapable of achieving success. I was unable to celebrate my accomplishments, because I truly believed I would NEVER amount to anything and I would NEVER be successful. This belief impacted how I saw myself and ultimately how I portrayed myself to others. It wasn't until I took the painful journey into the past to discover when my beliefs were birthed that I replaced these beliefs with my truths.

PART II: SELF-WORTH - As a result of the physical, verbal, and emotional abuse I experienced in three different relationships, I believed I was unworthy of love; thus I began accepting love no matter how it was given. I believed I was destined to be alone because I wasn't pretty enough, smart enough, or special enough to earn the love of a man. My darkest hour was when I allowed myself to be the other woman – believing that a part-time lover was all I could get. Fortunately, through my journey, I replaced my "clearance rack" mentality with a "couture" mindset.

PART III: SELF-CONFIDENCE – Because of several events throughout my teenage and young adult years, I wasn't confident in the way I dressed, my social skills (my ability to obtain true friendships), or my career. Due to my poor self-image and lack of self-worth, I believed that no one wanted to hear what I had to say. I wasn't intelligent or interesting, so why would anyone want to listen to me or even be around me? As part of my journey, I had to really get to know Lashana – my true essence and my values. I also had to understand and accept the parts of me that make me unique; including the way I dress, talk and think. Today I walk, talk, and dress like a BOSS, which is how God created me to be.

WHO SHOULD READ THIS BOOK

I wrote this book for anyone who has, is, or knows someone battling with low self-esteem. Most of my life, I dealt with the demon of self-hate alone; wearing masks to disguise my internal pain, seeking love from men when I didn't love myself, and suffering in private until the darkness became unbearable – where ending my life seemed like the only option. I want you to know that you don't have to deal with this alone. The demon of self-hate can and will be defeated.

As you take this journey with me, you will read about the events and people who bruised, damaged and destroyed my self-image, self-worth, and self-confidence. With each page, I hope you will see similarities in your past or current situation and realize that whatever the circumstance that impacted your self-esteem, YOU ARE NOT ALONE.

The pain I endured was unbearable, because there wasn't a pill or procedure that could take away the pain. I felt as if I had to keep my suffering a secret because most people dismissed this type of pain as something that could go away with a good night's rest or cup of tea. Then, there's the misconception that if you're intelligent, attractive or wealthy etc., you shouldn't have any problems. The combination of social biases and the "happiness myth" all but forced me to suffer in silence. My silence kept me in a state of depression and despair – almost to the brink of suicide.

Thank God, I can now chuckle at the ignorance of others; knowing firsthand that this type of pain isn't a consequence of external factors – beauty, success, material possessions, etc. The pain is within and can't be swept or wished away. It's usually the result of events, words and/or actions of loved ones, either in our distant or recent past, that have made us believe we're NOT ENOUGH – not pretty enough, smart enough, successful enough, etc.

I speak from experience when I say, "the pain is real." And although crippling at times, it doesn't have to last forever. The first step to healing is recognizing it; saying to yourself, "I suffer from low self-esteem." Now that you recognize it, you MUST be willing to do the work – taking the steps to uncover the people and/or event(s) that caused you to believe you aren't enough. Once you UNDERSTAND where the "stinking thinking" came from, then you MUST go through the process of forgiveness (yourself and others), renewing your mind (removing the negative beliefs with positive truths) and rebuilding yourself to become the person (the king or queen) God intended you to be.

Going through this process was a matter of life or death for me and now I can honestly say, "I WAKE UP FLAWLESS." My hope is that after reading this book, you will be empowered with the mental and emotional weapons needed to defeat the demon of self-hate, so that you too can wake up every morning knowing that you are FLAWLESS, too. **NOW LET'S BEGIN OUR JOURNEY!!!**

PART I
SELF-IMAGE

Death and life are in the power of the tongue...

PROVERBS 18:21

CHAPTER 1

THE JOURNEY BEGINS

How did I get to this place? A place where all I saw was darkness. My days and nights were spent wearing masks to hide my pain, fighting back the tears that were evidence of my feeling uncomfortable in my own skin, and contemplating how to end the pain once and for all. It took every ounce of energy I had to get through the workday. Putting on a facade and acting happy was draining – sometimes even impossible. In this place of darkness, I couldn't find the energy or the desire to interact with my family and friends. All I wanted to do was nestle myself in the bed, curl up in a ball, and go to sleep – until the pain subsided or forever.

The pain was like nothing I've ever experienced. My body felt heavy, unable to move. My joints were stiff much like your body's response to exercise after neglecting to stretch. My mind was weighed down by a dense, dark fog that hindered me from focusing, and the mental pain could only be described as menstrual pain on steroids. There wasn't any pill I could take and a cup of tea wouldn't subdue the pain (my mother's remedy for everything). The only way to find relief was to make myself go to sleep, FOREVER.

There was a part of me that knew I had to get help before my world went completely black. Contemplating the end was new and scary for me and this was when I realized help was no longer a want. It was a matter of life or death. The type of help I needed couldn't be found in a self-help book, speaking to my friends, or *just* going to church. I needed professional help. This realization forced me to assess my own biases around therapy.

Only "crazy" people went to therapy...right??? I now know this was wrong on so many levels. But at the time, it was difficult for me to change my mindset – a mindset culturally ingrained in my beliefs. This was until I found the courage to share my decision to consult a therapist with one of my dearest friends, Debra.

It was all in divine order, because like myself, she too, was in a dark space and researching therapists. God knows exactly what you need and when. God knew that I needed support and He also knew that I was a procrastinator and thus would never have taken the steps I needed to get help. In one conversation, the plan that saved my life was set in motion.

This was how God worked...On a Tuesday, I received a postcard from my employer's EAP provider promoting their mental health and wellness services. *Ok God, I got the hint.*

But I still wasn't completely sold on the idea of going to a therapist for help. So I saved the postcard and put it in a convenient place – my office – among several mountains of paper, folders and binders. Needless to say, I misplaced the postcard and conveniently forgot about my quest to seek help. That was until God once again intervened, forcing me to take action.

Days, weeks, and maybe a month passed since I received and misplaced the postcard from my EAP provider. During this span of time, I purposely consumed myself with work. I thought if I stayed busy and maintained my act of normalcy, I would be okay and then, this too, would pass. My thinking was completely flawed. Not only was I not getting the help I desperately needed, my busyness kept me from noticing that I was falling further and further into a state of despair.

Almost four weeks to the day I first received the postcard from my EAP provider, Debra gave me the contact information of several therapists. Still skeptical, I reluctantly researched a few of the sites, so I could honestly tell her I did something. But my search was quickly interrupted when I became frightened by the thought of trusting someone with my most private thoughts – trusting someone whom I didn't know to literally save my life. The more I allowed my thoughts to consume me, the more my anxiety grew...ugh.

I was all but ready to abandon the whole idea of working with a therapist, but God wasn't having it. Once again, He stepped in by subtly nudging Debra to call to check on my progress and to share the contact information of a therapist she found to be very reputable. Equipped with the name and number of a therapist, I no longer had an excuse. As soon as hung up with Debra, I picked up the phone, dialed the therapist's number, and started my journey to healing.

Still filled with my biases around therapy, I had to mentally prepare for my first visit. Even as I walked through the office doors, I wasn't quite convinced that a therapist wouldn't be anything more than a complete waste of my time and money. I told myself that I was just going to "check her out," not share too much, and determine if another visit was necessary. Well, like with most things in life, my first visit didn't go according to plan. One visit turned into a three-year therapist-patient relationship.

◄═╬═ ═╬═►

The office wasn't quite as I pictured it. I was expecting a room much like I saw on television – an office-like room with one big chair and a chaise for the patient to lie on. On the contrary, this office was quaint, soothing, and set up more like a small living or sitting room. The environment made me feel comfortable and less intimidated.

My therapist was a tall, white lady full of energy, with a demeanor that made me trust her immediately. Comfortable and feeling quite relaxed, it didn't take long before I was sharing my innermost thoughts with a tissue in hand to wipe my crying eyes. Somewhere in our conversation, she asked me to describe myself. The words that poured out of my mouth made her sad – noticeable by the sadness in her eyes and the way she shifted her body in her chair. My description went a little something like this...

"I'm a black woman; somewhat smart, but not intelligent; cute, but not pretty or sexy; not very nice; not the life of anyone's party, hence I don't get many invites; cheap and selfish; a homebody and I assume there's something wrong with me since I've yet to have a healthy relationship with a man. I can't keep a man and the love I've given has yet to be reciprocated by another. I think this is all for now."

With a saddened look on her face, my therapist asked why I described myself as such, and did I remember when I formed this vision of myself? The questions brought me to uncontrollable tears. My vision of myself was my little secret. I thought it, owned it, but never voiced it to anyone.

It's true. There is power in words. The minute I started describing myself, it became real. It was at that moment that I truly felt the pain of never feeling good enough, pretty enough, smart enough...

I first answered the question with a shrug of my shoulders and in a small whimper, I whispered, "I don't know."

I thought my answer would put an end to this topic – at least for that session. However, my therapist was on to my little plan. Her response to my, "I don't know" was another question and another question until through deep sobs I answered her, "I think it has something to do with what people told me when I was a child."

I was just as shocked as she was when the words came pouring out of my mouth. It was as if her insistent questioning subconsciously brought me back to my childhood – to the time and place where my self-image was shattered. And in that moment, I was transformed to a time and place where the words and thoughts of others shaped the broken woman she saw before her...

CHAPTER 2
MOMMY DEAREST

"I love you, but I don't like you," my mother shouted to me.

Her words hurt like a thousand paper cuts, causing sharp pains through my heart with each and every syllable. I don't remember the first time my mother uttered the words that once shaped my fragile self-image, but I do remember how I felt each and every time she expressed her utter disapproval of me as a person.

The chain of events that prompted my mother's verbal attack escapes me. I don't remember what I said or did to make her say the words, "I don't like you," but I do recall her anger was fueled by me not doing, saying, or acting a certain way. In other words, I wasn't living up to my mother's expectations. I wasn't the child she wanted me to be.

To be honest, I don't think I ever lived up to my mother's expectations. When I was younger, she wanted me to be this submissive, docile, angelic little girl instead of the depressed, smart-mouthed child that I was. As I got older, she wanted me to be unconditionally loving and selfless – possessing the characteristics of one of those perfect daughters on television. Most of my life, I tried to live up to her expectations, although failing miserably. My trying to be the "perfect daughter" and my mother never accepting me for who I was diminished my self-image and damaged any possibility of a healthy mother-daughter relationship.

I was born the daughter of an unwed teenager who was pregnant at the age of eighteen, without a high school diploma and no immediate plans for the future. It is said that birth is a blessing, however, my birth was not welcomed with balloons or cigars. My introduction into the world was seen more as a burden to society's financial structure rather than a bundle of joy. I can assume that my mother's decision to have me was very difficult, for my entrance into the world presented her with many financial and social challenges. She was no longer a carefree teenager, dating boys and enjoying her last years before adulthood. She was now a mother, responsible for the well being of someone other than herself.

Although it wasn't easy, my mother made sure I had a roof over my head, food to eat, and clothes on my back. And although she didn't officially graduate from high school, she instilled in me the importance of education. I don't know if it was the stress of raising a child while merely a child herself, or if it was the realization of unfilled dreams that contributed to her dislike of me. But whatever the justification, it didn't change the emotional and mental anguish I endured for most of my life.

I love you, but I do not like you.

Hearing these words from one of my classmates would have been devastating for a moment, but hearing these words from my own mother was enough to make me want to die. If my own mother didn't like me, then who would? This very question was the catalyst for my damaged self-image. It was as if my mind was sent into a state of paranoia in which I was flooded with negative thoughts – *your friends don't like you; your boyfriend(s) only want you for one thing; no one will ever really want to be your friend.* My mother's damaging words were just the invite the demon of self-hate needed to make itself a resident in my life.

As much as I wanted to think her words didn't have an impact on me, I realized after hearing her words, "I don't like you," I yearned for my mother's acceptance. I wanted to be the person she loved and also liked, but I didn't really know how. So I found myself on an impossible quest to be the person I thought my mother wanted me to be.

With each passing day, I shed characteristics, qualities and behaviors that were innate to the person God created, hoping to become someone people would like – most importantly my mother. I felt as if I was auditioning for a part in a play for which I didn't have a script. I didn't know what to say or how to act. All I knew was that whatever the role, I couldn't be myself.

Wearing masks and pretending to be someone else made it difficult for me to develop true friendships. Usually the beginning of every relationship consists of getting to know the other person – sharing experiences, thoughts and emotions. Unfortunately, the girls I befriended never got the opportunity to get to know me. I acted the way I thought they wanted me to act, imitated their style of dress, and shared only the things I thought they wanted to hear.

When asked who I was as a child, I often found myself holding back tears, for I really couldn't answer the question. I was a stranger to myself and didn't know who I was. I remember there were several occasions when my mother told me that I was mean, selfish, inconsiderate, and unloving. I can't believe that I was such a horrible child, and so drastically different from the person I am today. I questioned whether my mother's opinion of me was a true depiction of my authentic self or the result of her never truly understanding me.

If I was actually the person my mother thought I was, today I would be malicious and unkind (mean), self-centered and egotistical (selfish), insensitive and uncaring (inconsiderate), heartless and unfeeling (unloving). But I wonder if her perception of me would have changed if she knew that everything I did or said – up until just recently – was in hope of pleasing her. All I ever wanted was for my mother to like me.

My mother often compared me to others, asking why I couldn't be more like this person or that person. Growing up, my cousin, April, who I lived with, was very timid and selfless. If I wasn't being compared to her, then I was blatantly asked about my many character flaws. "Why are you so insensitive, selfish, mean, or rude?" Oh yeah, I was also considered cheap because of my unhealthy relationship with money. I held on to every penny I earned in anticipation of a "rainy day." It was as if winning my mother's acceptance was a losing battle. Her perception of me was so tarnished, it was impossible for me to ever win her over.

"You should be more like your cousin," my mother would say when I wasn't being the sweet and docile child she obviously wanted. Imagine hearing this over and over again. The first time, you may have ignored it. The second time, you may have sucked your teeth, rolled your eyes and moved on. But the third, fourth and twentieth time you heard it may have been hard to ignore. Every time she said it, I wanted to cry, wondering why I couldn't just be me? Why was I not good enough?

Once the tears subsided, I wanted badly to yell to my mother, "What's so good about April? What makes her so perfect?" But instead, I mumbled some curse words under my breath and retreated either to my room or the quiet place in my head. That must be when I learned how to tune people out.

Growing up, my cousin, April, was considered timid, selfless and quiet. Whereas I was – or at least I was perceived to be – sarcastic, mean, selfish and often too grown for my own good. My cousin and I were two different people, but were both good children in our own way. Today, children are praised for having "personality" or being unique, but when

I was growing up, my uniqueness was considered a character flaw and was neither praised nor appreciated. Through my mother's words, I was made acutely aware that being me wasn't enough, thus causing me to believe that I needed to be someone other than myself – creating an internal struggle.

As my mother commanded, I tried to be more like my cousin, but my attempts went unnoticed. Each time I tried, my efforts backfired and made matters worse, much like this one particular time I still remember to this day.

I don't remember the specific occasion – it may have been Mother's Day. All I remember is that I tried to do something nice for my mother – an act I thought would surely please her – only to make her upset and increase her disdain for me.

April and I were given a dozen roses to give to our mothers. I was so excited to get home and present my mother with the beautiful, red roses. I must have skipped all the way home in anticipation of seeing her smiling face. But to my disappointment, when I got home, she wasn't anywhere to be found. I was forced to wait, and wait, and wait, listening for her keys in the front door. With every minute, my anxiety increased and I grew impatient. I couldn't wait to finally win my mother's affection.

Anxious and needing to do something to calm my nerves, I took one or two of the roses and sprinkled the rose petals on her bed and put the other roses in a vase. During the act, I envisioned the women on television and how they were always happy when a man scattered rose petals at their feet. Therefore, I thought my mother would surely appreciate the gesture. Boy, was I wrong.

When I heard my mother's keys in the door, I could hardly subdue my excitement. I ran to greet her as she entered her room. I had to see the look on her face when she saw the nice surprise I had for her. But my mother's emotionless face quickly informed me that she did NOT like my surprise. Before she totally went off on me, she took the time and energy to call and ask my aunt about her roses, inquiring if April presented the roses the same way. My mother went as far as to comment, "I know April didn't do something as stupid as this. And now I have to clean this shit up."

Satisfied that her anger was justified, my mother went on a long tirade. "Why didn't you just put the roses in a vase? Why did you make a mess for me to clean up?" Her disappointment with what I thought was an act of love ignited my sadness. After apologizing, I held back my tears and ran to my room, and from that day on, I never tried to surprise my mother again.

That wasn't the last time my attempt to act more like my cousin backfired, which created a deep sense of disappointment and frustration within me. I wanted to be the daughter my mother could be proud of – someone more like my cousin – but it seemed the more I tried, the more my mother disliked me.

Even to this day, my good deeds go unnoticed. Every time I don't do something, it's remembered forever – not offering to pick her up from the airport when I already knew she made arrangements; or not offering to pay for a trip I thought she decided not to go on; or not purchasing a gift or giving money when she felt I should have offered. And it's not surprising that my kind gestures – birthday gifts, Mother's Day gifts etc. – go unnoticed. When it comes to my mother, I can't win for losing.

"You are so mean and rude," my mother would say in a voice that expressed her utter disgust with me. This was part of her famous speech whenever we had company and I was less than cordial. Being uncomfortable in my own skin and untrusting of the world around me made it difficult for me to be the social butterfly my mother wanted me to be. When adult company came over, I would barely speak. Sometimes, as soon as I heard the doorbell ring, I would sequester myself in my room, where I would listen to music or write in my journal.

It was as if the mere sight of an adult immediately brought me to a state of overwhelming discomfort and unhappiness. Based on my experience with adults – my mother, her friends, Charles and Bernard, my teachers and my grandfather (I'll go into more details later) – it's no wonder why I chose to stay away from adults. I could have been enjoying a movie or playing my favorite game – smiling from ear to ear – and as soon as I felt the presence of an adult, my disposition would be negatively altered. My smile would turn into a frown and I would immediately feel the need to retreat to the solitude of my bedroom.

I loved my bedroom. It was my safe haven. My room was one of the largest rooms in the house, situated off of the kitchen and right next to the bathroom. You could say my bedroom was conveniently located.

Inside these four walls is where I was happy. I had my boom box on which I played my tapes – escaping my reality through music. My color television allowed me to live vicariously through the lives of the characters in shows like *The Cosby Show*, *A Different World*, and *Different Strokes*. There was also my telephone – a necessity for any teenage girl. Although my favorite gadget in my room, my telephone was also the most costly. As a lesson in responsibility, my mother agreed to give me a phone with the mutual understanding that I would pay the bill with my allowance. A small price to pay for happiness.

You may be wondering how I was able to obtain these luxuries (boom box, television, gaming system etc.). Let's just say things were always "falling off the back of a truck."

As a child, I didn't know how to protect myself from adults' harsh words. I was raised to always respect my elders. So how was I supposed to respond to an adult who told me I would never go anywhere in life or who said with a straight face, "I didn't know you were smart enough to read at a higher level"?

Their words destroyed my self-esteem and kept me a prisoner of my own internal struggle. With every harsh word, I was flooded with emotions – angry because I was unable to retaliate, hurt because I was humiliated and degraded, and saddened because no one came to my defense. If they were my peers, I would have countered their remarks with a sarcastic rebuttal or better yet, the finger. However, in an attempt to remain respectful, I was rendered helpless. Thus, the only way I knew how to protect myself was to hide away in my room.

I longed to be a part of the world outside of my room, but I was overcome with fear. I wanted to socialize more, but I was angry at adults for never coming to save me, leaving me in the big bad world to defend myself. I was a child in a fragile emotional state. I didn't understand what I was experiencing, nor did I know how to fix it. All I knew was that something wasn't right, but I didn't know what.

Since I was too young to make sense of it all, I looked to adults for the answers. So although I didn't want to believe it, their perception became my reality and I accepted that I was "mean" and assumed the characteristics that went with it. I wasn't born mean and I didn't want to be mean, but there wasn't any other logical explanation for my behavior – hiding in my room and not being social. The more I heard, "You're mean and anti-social," the easier it was for me to transform into the person they thought I was, thereby losing the person I was born to be.

CHAPTER 3

HIGHER LEARNING

"You will never amount to anything. You will never be more than another statistic – pregnant at the age of eighteen and on welfare."

Close your eyes and imagine being a small helpless child and hearing these words from your mother's closest friends or even worse, members of your own family. As a child, I didn't understand why the adults in my life, whom I trusted and were supposed to protect me, consistently told me that I was a failure who wasn't going to amount to anything when I grew up. The words sting today just as much as they did so many years ago.

My success, or lack thereof, was a recurring topic of discussion. Sometimes, the discussion lasted a few minutes, but there were times when the discussion seemed like it went on forever. Any conversation would seem like forever if you're the one put in the spotlight and worst of all, you're unable to defend yourself.

So unfortunately, I heard the words, "going to be a failure," and "not going to succeed" more times than I can count. As a defense mechanism, I erased many of these conversations from my memory. I hate to think of my emotional state had I remembered every negative word that was spoken from the mouths of certain adults in my life. However, there was one conversation that has been imprinted in my memory like a tattoo and has been nearly impossible for me to forget.

Growing up, my bedroom was right next to the kitchen and dining room. With each room being in such close proximity, it was easy for me to hear adult conversations about topics that were far too grown for my young adolescent ears. It was equally difficult for me to ignore conversations where I was the topic of discussion. As a child, I must have listened to hundreds of conversations that today, I would deem inappropriate for any child to hear. But none of the conversations emotionally scarred me like this one conversation that took place right outside my bedroom door.

With a bewildered look on my face, I remained completely still as I listened with my ear pressed to my bedroom door while my mother's friends, Charles and Bernard, debated the reason for my inevitably unsuccessful future. They debated whether my failure would be due to the demise of the public school system, which would result in my inability to receive an acceptable education and therefore make it unlikely for me to get a decent paying job in the future. OR, was my foretold failure due to my infatuation with boys, which meant I would start having sex before high school and get pregnant before graduation. OR, was I just a product of my environment and as such, possessed with a poverty mentality – mentally incapable of advancing any further than the surrounding blocks of my neighborhood.

I couldn't believe they would condemn me to a life of failure before my twenty-first birthday, or better yet, my high school graduation. I was only a child, for goodness sake. A child with nothing but possibilities, who could have been anything she wanted to be with the right guidance. A child who needed the adults in her life to support and protect her; not adults who eagerly awaited the "train wreck" they foretold as my life.

Tears streamed down my little face as I continued to listen to their hurtful conversation. Because of the close proximity of my room, they must have known I could hear every word, which confirmed they were trifling individuals who didn't care about crushing the hopes and dreams of a young innocent child. With the volume of their voices almost at a loud scream, it was as if they wanted me to hear every negative, dream-crushing word.

Nevertheless, they continued on with their conversation as if they had the answer to world peace. You would have thought they had PhD's on the socioeconomic influences of children born and raised in the ghetto. Although they had the right to their opinion, the presence of an impressionable child was not the place to voice it.

Charles and Bernard discussed at great lengths how they witnessed my obsession with boys, and in their "expert" opinion, this kind of behavior could only lead to one thing – sex, then babies, and ultimately a lifetime on public assistance. As if a woman who has a baby at an early age can't succeed in life – as if having a baby removes any opportunity of happiness. They were ignorant and limited in their thinking.

With the right mindset, support and determination, a person can do anything they put their mind to. In my opinion, they also spent way too much time on the difference between public and private school curricula. And since both men sent their children to private schools, they considered themselves the authorities on this topic.

Bernard sarcastically stated, "I heard her mother mention something about her reading on a high school level."

Charles quickly discredited my mother's alleged statement with his response, "In public school? Reading on a high school level only means she's reading at her current grade level, which really means she's behind. The longer she stays in public school, the longer she will remain on or below average, thus never having a chance of a successful future."

Bernard agreed with a hearty chuckle and then commented, "Hell, at the rate she's going, she shouldn't even worry about her grades and join that co-op thing offered in the local high schools. With her little public school education, it probably would be best if she gave up on the idea of college altogether."

At this point in the conversation, my hopes and dreams were fading away. I wondered why I should even try to get good grades in school. Based on their "expert" opinions, I was destined for failure and there was not much I could do to stop it.

I couldn't take it anymore. My face was full of dry and fresh tears, my eyes swollen and bloodshot red. The intensity and the length of time they spent on this topic was one of the reasons I vividly remember this conversation. But the reason this conversation was permanently imprinted in my mind is because this was the first time I started believing I was nothing and was NEVER going to be successful.

After ten minutes – or what seemed like an eternity – I left them to continue their disturbing discussion and fully retreated to the comfort of my room. It was within those walls that I allowed the tears that were drowning my eyes to flow. I contemplated their rationale and tried to make sense of it all. Was what they said true? They were adults and should know more than me, who was only in elementary school at the time.

But if I allowed myself to believe what they said, then I would never really know my true potential. I was a child and didn't know how to process all of it, so I did what children do – I allowed my anger to fuel my motivation. "They think they're so smart. I'll show them." But although their words fueled my achieving good grades in school, the damage was already done. The unfortunate victim of that conversation was my self-image – broken, fragile, and on the verge of destruction.

It is said that the power of life or death is in the tongue. This is so true, for with every discouraging word spoken out the mouths of Charles and Bernard, my self-esteem, confidence, and self-image were destroyed. Many people don't realize how powerful their words are, but continue to tell a child they are stupid and they will begin to believe. Unfortunately, if you tell a child enough times, they will begin to perpetuate this self- image, and a child who once had the potential to succeed is talked into a life of mediocrity.

A coping mechanism for people who battle with low self-esteem is to overcompensate in an area in their life over which they feel they have control. I just recently learned this. For me, this area was my education. I was always in the top percentile of my grade – despite what Charles and Bernard thought. I was in honors classes and never received anything less than a B+ in grade school, except for physical education. I validated myself through academics. How could there be anything wrong with me if I was able to do so well in school? I convinced myself, and others, that I was a well-adjusted child.

Unfortunately, my grades were not enough to sway the opinions of those that didn't believe in me. To Charles and Bernard, my grades were a clear indication of how the public school system fails inner city youths – giving A's to students who didn't possess the basic fundamentals to be competitive with their counterparts in private school or affluent suburban schools. Let them tell it, I was just another child reaping the academic benefits of a failed school system. It never occurred to them that maybe, just maybe, I was an intelligent child who deserved the A's that were given by my teachers. It never dawned on them that I could have been destined for greatness, if only someone believed in me.

Charles and Bernard were adults, which meant as a child I had to respect them. But fortunately, I only had to endure their negative banter until the end of their stay. Needless to say, every time they visited, I couldn't wait until the front door closed behind them and I was able to leave my room and walk around my house without being ridiculed and humiliated.

Charles and Bernard's conversations were enough to scar my fragile self-image, but when I learned that my grandfather shared the same sentiments, I was overcome with feelings of despair, sadness, and anger. A few days after I graduated from high school, my grandfather stopped by (since he chose not to attend my graduation; a topic for a later date) to tell me that he was happy that I didn't get pregnant and drop out of school.

I could only imagine the confused look I had on my face as my grandfather praised me for not becoming a statistic; all the while failing to address my accomplishment of graduating high school with honors and being accepted into a university.

I've never told anyone this (and if you ask me I will deny it) but unbeknownst to me at the time, I used my anger towards my mother's friends, my grandfather, and all the others who didn't believe in me, to fuel my drive to graduate from college. Although my self-image was broken, I was relentless in my pursuit of a college degree. I couldn't give those assholes the satisfaction of being right about my "unsuccessful" future. Hence, the days when I didn't believe in myself – and there were many – I persevered, motivated by the fact that I had to prove them wrong. I had to get my degree no matter the cost. As the saying goes…I let my haters be my motivators.

CHAPTER 4

BAD TEACHER

My academic foundation was received in both the public and private school systems. One might assume that the quality of education was greatest in private school, but on the contrary, I was most challenged in my honors classes in public school. This comment would give Charles and Bernard a heart attack. The private school I attended was more concerned with my mother's affiliation with the church – or lack thereof – than my education.

I attended private school for all of the fourth grade and half of the fifth. When I first enrolled, it took a while for me to get acclimated, so my being advanced in my studies was not an issue at the time. However, once I established my group of friends and got accustomed to the parochial environment,

I started really focusing on my schoolwork. At this time, it became apparent that I was far more advanced than many of my classmates.

By the time I entered the fourth grade, my reading and math were on a high school level based on standardized exams. You would have thought the school would have been inclined to offer academic solutions to keep me challenged, such as having me skip a grade or allowing me to attend advanced classes. But since my mother wasn't and was never going to be a member of their affiliated church, neither of these options was made available to me. So instead of getting the education I required, I was given additional textbooks and told to study on my own. How's that for private school education? It was all about dollars and cents.

We all know that if a child is not challenged in school, they will begin to act out, and act out was exactly what I did. I finished my work before everyone else, so I felt it was only right to strike up conversations with my friends, pass notes, or tell jokes. My behavior didn't make me very popular with the teachers; or shall I say this made my somewhat blemished reputation even worse. Yes, in the fourth grade, I already had a reputation. The sad part was, my reputation wasn't started by jealous classmates. It was birthed out of the mouths of immature teachers.

In the third grade, I was not only academically advanced. I was also physically advanced. At the time, I was already a "C" cup, and for this reason, I was already labeled by the teachers as being "fast." They say, "be careful what you wish for." I laugh at myself now, but I may have played a minor part in my advanced development...

In the first grade, I was "flat-chested," but I dreamed of having something to fill my Wonder Woman Underoos bra. Although most of the girls in my class didn't have anything resembling a bump, I wanted my breasts to grow more than anything in the world.

In one of my favorite childhood books, *Dear God, It's Me Margaret*, by Judy Blume, the main character, Margaret, thought by repeating the words, "I must, I must, I must increase my bust," that her breasts would miraculously grow. It didn't work for Margaret, but I didn't see any harm in trying it myself. So I made this chant part of my daily routine for a week. Needless to say, I was very disappointed when after a week of "hard work," I was just as flat-chested as when I started.

Desperate to have breasts, I decided it would be a good idea to stuff my bra with tissue. This was NOT the brightest idea I've ever had. Oh, this idea was bad on so many levels, and since I have evidence of my foolish plan, I really wish I'd just allowed nature to take its course.

The day we were supposed to take school pictures, I thought I had the best plan ever. My plan was to stuff my bra with tissue, showing the world in my pictures that I had breasts. What was I thinking? I should have forfeited my plan when I noticed my friend, who was supposed to be my partner in crime, removed her tissue right before the cameraman called her name. It wasn't until I took the picture that I realized the consequences of what I had done. Not only was I embarrassed – I wasn't skilled at stuffing a bra, so let's just say I was a little lopsided – but I became acutely aware that I was going to receive the worst beating ever. And if that wasn't bad enough, I had these pictures to remind me of my master plan for the rest of my life.

Be careful what you wish for. Not even two years later, my breasts didn't stop growing. It turned out that the breasts I so desired became the object of much humiliation, physical pain, and a source of contention for my fragile self-image. My breasts and I had a love-hate relationship. The words of others shaped how I thought of myself, and to me, I was nothing more than big breasts and a smile. And although having big breasts with a small frame made for chronic back pains, wardrobe challenges, as well as indentations in my shoulders, I allowed myself to believe that without my large breasts, I wasn't attractive and had nothing to offer a man.

I thought I needed large breasts to get men, but I was frustrated and unhappy every time I went shopping. Wearing cute little tops was out of the question...bras in my size didn't come with low or zigzag backs. Wearing dresses was nearly impossible unless I wanted to pay for alterations – size 2-6 on the bottom and 8-12 on the top. Last time I checked, dresses only came in one size. Oh and those little nighties looked a hot mess when your breasts hung much lower than the designated cups.

The discussion of a breast reduction was brought up several times by doctors, but I wouldn't entertain the idea because without my breasts, I would be nothing – unattractive, not sexy, and undesirable to men. I didn't want to be invisible, so I endured the physical pain and wardrobe issues for years.

This was further perpetuated by my many failed relationships with men. I believed I was able to get a man because of my breasts, but I couldn't keep a man because once in a relationship, they realized that I was socially challenged, insecure, and unhappy...I was nothing more than my breasts.

As I mentioned, in the fourth grade, I was already wearing a C cup. I had the breast size of a grown woman and the mind of a child. I didn't really understand what was going on with my body. I didn't know that I had to dress and carry myself differently – my shirts were a little tighter, certain activities were off limits (like Double Dutch), oh and the pain. No one ever tells you about the pain you endure in your shoulders and back when you have to carry around two coconuts.

And no one prepares you for the stares and the snide remarks that come with having large breasts and a small frame at a very young age. I especially wasn't prepared for the torment I received from adults who were too stupid to realize that no matter what age my body portrayed, I was still a fragile child. Unfortunately, I had to learn at a very young age that my physical appearance was going to cause me problems with girls my own age, as well as adults. I first learned this lesson while I was in private school. In the fourth grade, I wasn't ready for this life lesson.

When I first learned of the school's annual field trip, I was so excited because for the first time, we were able to wear our street clothes. Being allowed to shed our boring, private school uniforms for something a bit more stylish was like being released from prison for a day. I convinced my mother to take me shopping in search of the perfect outfit. After several hours of walking through the mall, I finally had my outfit – navy blue pants that fit me tight around my hips and thighs, a light blue and navy, cut-off top that stopped just above my belly button, a red studded belt and some red shoes. What can I say? It was the 80's.

On the day of the event, I got dressed like I was preparing for a photo shoot – like a model on the runway. I viewed myself in the mirror from every angle just to make sure I looked equally good from the back, side, and front. I was in my own supermodel world, so I didn't notice the look the female van driver gave me when I walked onto the school van. Possibly clue number one that my wardrobe choice was too much for the Christian school. But once again, I was a child and I didn't know any better and I damn sure wasn't experienced enough to pick up on subtle cues – like the nasty look the van driver gave me.

I entered the school with all the confidence in the world. I thought I was too cute and no one could tell me any different. Unfortunately, by the end of the day, my confidence was deflated much like a balloon at the end of a party. Based on the rolling of their eyes and their whispers, it was apparent that the teachers didn't approve of my attire. But instead of handling the situation like mature adults, they proceeded to make remarks in front of my peers like, "Look at what she's wearing. Her outfit is a little inappropriate for a field day." And, "Her breasts are way too big for that shirt."

That day, I was called all sorts of derogatory names. Worst of all, I remember them making a comment about me being the product of the ghetto, mumbling something like, "The fruit doesn't fall far from the tree" – referring to my mother as a heathen since she wasn't a member of the affiliated church. They were such hypocrites. Needless to say, their remarks did nothing for my already bruised self-image. Once again, I was made to feel like I was nothing and would never amount to anything.

The sadness I felt after hearing the words from my teachers was crippling. I wanted to be invisible. All I wanted to do was curl up in a ball and cry. I thought I could control my emotions until I got home, but since they found it necessary to tear down my self-image in front of my classmates, my sadness was quickly coupled with anger. Their words ignited such anger inside of me that I lost all self-control, and as the tears rolled down my face, the curse words poured out of my mouth. I guess this is the part where I should mention that growing up, I had an attitude problem – I was mad at the world. I've come a long way since those days, but I still have a bit of a sarcastic mouth...I'm just me!

As you can imagine, my cursing didn't go over well with the teachers. As a result, my mother was called to the school for a meeting in the principal's office. Now that I think about it, my mother's presence was more of a formality, because prior to the meeting, they conspired to tell the story from their perspective. During the meeting there wasn't any mention of what they said about me in front of my classmates. Their version of the story went a little something like this...

> *We noticed her attire was distracting the other students, especially the boys. So one of us decided to pull her aside to inform her of her poor wardrobe choice and to politely ask her if she had a change of clothes or if her mother could bring her another shirt. This is when she started getting sassy, raising her voice when I told her she wouldn't be able to participate in field day until she got another shirt. Lashana then started using four-letter words – words I don't dare repeat – being disrespectful and causing a scene in front of the other students.*

The only truth to their story was that they did voice their disapproval of my outfit – in front of the entire school – and I was disrespectful. But they failed to mention how I was provoked. I couldn't believe my ears. After they told their tainted story, everyone including my mother, agreed I was in the wrong and as part of my punishment, I was sent home on three days suspension.

Although there is never an excuse for being rude to adults, I never told my mother my side of the story. I never once told her that the teachers who were supposed to educate and protect me called me all sorts of "hoes" and "sluts." I didn't tell my mother because I didn't trust her to protect me against my teachers, since she never stopped Charles and Bernard from talking about me in my own home. After all, those teachers were adults just like Charles and Bernard who were allowed to degrade and destroy my self-image.

Fortunately, after that incident, it wasn't long before I left private school and returned back to the public school system. But for the days, weeks and months leading up to my departure, the teachers took full advantage of this time, going out of their way to let me know they didn't care for me. I would hear the teachers whispering and laughing at me as I walked through the halls; pointing in my direction and every once in a while murmuring the words, "ho" or "slut."

This was a lonely time for me. I felt as if the world was turning against me and I didn't have anywhere or anyone to turn to. Even my so-called friends started acting weird, so I couldn't talk to them. I was only in the fourth grade and already my trust and respect for adults was tainted...I was alone.

I was only a child. I couldn't quite comprehend what was going on. Why were the adults in my life so mean and hurtful? Unable to make any sense of it, I added my teachers' snide remarks and negative comments to all the other harsh words I endured from my mother's friends. I had an imaginary war chest filled with the devastating words, my emotions, my deflated self-image, and my crushed dreams. Over the years, my war chest turned into a closet and then into a small room. As my war chest became larger, my self-image slowly evaporated to the point it was non-existent.

CHAPTER 5

CLASS ACT

"If she doesn't stop chasing boys, she is destined to be a teenage mom, never graduating from high school."

I was furious when I heard my teacher say this to my mother, as if they were girlfriends and she was "helping a sistah out." It was parent-teacher night for goodness sake. Shouldn't my teacher keep the discussion about my grades, my perfect attendance, and how I was an overall good student? No, she thought it was a better use of time to focus on the one area I felt was none of her damn business...my interest in boys. Little did they know, my interest in boys was less about hormones and more about my need to fill a void that existed due to the absence of my father.

Don't worry – I'll go into more detail about this in later chapters.

Sitting there listening to my teacher and my mother talk about my love life was painful. The longer I sat there, the angrier I became. My teacher went on and on about how my relationship with a boy in my class named David – who was my boyfriend (whatever that meant in the sixth grade) – was unhealthy and affecting my studies. I knew that whether true or false, the mere mention of something or someone affecting my grades would send my mother into a frenzy. There were two areas my mother was very passionate about – education and honesty. She despised liars.

What I feared the most happened as soon as we left the school. My mother told me that I had to end my relationship with David immediately. This meant no more talking on the phone, physical contact of any kind, and no more walking home together. Why didn't she just kill me already? I thought I would die without a boyfriend. Who was going to give me the attention and affection I so craved? Who was going to make me complete by filling the hole in my heart?

Although I never forgave my sixth grade teacher for convincing my mother that I had an unhealthy attraction to boys, she was not the only one who felt the need to voice their opinion on the topic. It was rumored that my teacher from the third grade, Miss Martin, felt the need to add her two cents, telling one of my neighbors, who was like one of my second mothers, that I was boy crazy and headed for disaster. Needless to say, it didn't take long for this information to get back to my mother. It was official. I was a "fast" little girl who was on the path to being a statistic. There was no way my mother was going to allow me to speak to a boy, let alone have a boyfriend. I wished Miss Martin kept her two cents to herself, for she, nor my sixth grade teacher understood how I needed – or at least I thought at the time – to feel liked by boys.

As I previously mentioned, my mother's friends shared the same sentiment, suggesting that I would be pregnant by the age of eighteen. My own grandfather had the nerve to tell me on the day I graduated high school that he thought I would be a teenage mother and he was proud of me for not getting pregnant before completing high school. It's sad to say that this may have been the nicest thing my grandfather ever said to me.

In my opinion, my grandfather was a cowardly man who allowed his wife to alienate him from his children and grandchildren. He lived in the house next door to ours, and in the span of ten years, I don't remember spending any quality time with him. I have no memory of him attending any of my graduations (I had four if you count my graduation from kindergarten), or events at school, or having any positive presence in my life.

For years, I internalized his actions. I often overheard my classmates talking about their grandparents with such adoration, while the mere thought of my grandfather brought on tears of anger and sadness. A grandparent's love should be unconditional, however, I couldn't earn or buy my grandfather's love, which further exacerbated my need to find love in the arms of boys.

It's sad that adults thought of me as some kind of walking hormone. They thought my interest in boys was the result of an overactive sex drive. This could not have been further from the truth. My interest in boys had more to do with my NEED to be loved rather than my need for loving. My self-esteem was shattered, for which they were partially to blame. The only way I knew how to cope was to find comfort in the attention and affection from the opposite sex.

CHAPTER 6

THE PATH TO HEALING: SELF-IMAGE

The motivation for me is them telling
me what I could not be, oh well. ~ JAY Z
BLUEPRINT 3

I t has taken me a long time to realize that my mother loves me, although I may never live up to her expectations. And you know what? I'm okay with that. I've finally accepted who I am. I now surround myself with people who appreciate me for my authentic self and those who expect me to be any more or less than who I am have been given their "walking papers." To get to this place wasn't easy and didn't happen overnight. There were several times when I wanted to give up, stop reliving the past, and stop doing the work to rebuild my self-image. But I remembered the dark place I was in when I first started this journey and I knew that quitting wasn't an option, for I would never go back to that place again.

My path to acceptance began with one question from my therapist, "Why do you think there's something wrong with you?"

My answer was, "Because THEY said so."

She then asked, "What did they say that you accepted and now BELIEVE about yourself?"

This is when I rambled off, "I'm unsocial, mean, difficult to get along with, cheap, unlikeable, stupid and unsuccessful."

The next part of the conversation was so profound that it changed my way of thinking forever. My therapist then asked, "Who are THEY, and what makes THEM an expert?"

I pondered this for what seemed like ten minutes and it dawned on me that for so long, I allowed the perception of others to dictate my behaviors, thoughts and personality. Their perception became my reality. So much so that I didn't know who I was. After this conversation, she guided me through a series of steps and exercises to help me rebuild my self-image.

INSIGHTS I learned on my journey:

I. IDENTIFY THE PROBLEM. My journey into the past was not intentionally meant to evoke unwanted emotions, but was a necessary voyage to help me understand the source of my never-ending battle with the demon of self-hate. In order for me to defeat it, I needed to comprehend its existence. How was it possible for the demon of self-hate to take up permanent residence in every area of my life?

II. DETERMINE THE ROOT OF THE "STINKING THINKING". For years, because of the negative words of others and the lack of acceptance from my mother, I lived in a state of confusion. I didn't like who I was and I didn't know who I should be. Who did I need to be in order to gain their love and approval? Instead of asking, "Why don't I love myself?" I was more focused on becoming the person others wanted me to be. The demon of self-hate was able to infiltrate my life in such a way that I rejected the concept that I didn't need to change. God didn't make any mistakes. I was fine just the way I was.

III. CHANGE YOUR MIDSET; RENEW YOUR MIND. As I've mentioned previously, I've read and followed the principles outlined in several self-help books and have found myself frustrated when the outcome was always the same – my self-love still remained non-existent.

It was not until I was able to truly SEE MYSELF that I was able to dispel the negative images I'd carried around for so many years. First, I had to ask myself, what made other people experts, such that I allowed them to alter my perception and opinion of myself. My mother's friends, teachers, and family members were all human and were not made any differently or any better than I. So why was it that I believed what they said about me, instead of accepting what I knew to be true?

IV. REPLACE NEGATIVE BELIEFS WITH TRUTHS. "You will never amount to anything but another statistic." These words may have had some validity to a child who was unaware of what the future held, but as an adult who beat all odds and overcame many obstacles, these words hold no truth. My graduation from high school was a testament to what I would accomplish. Hell, my academic career all but said, "kiss my ass" to all those who thought I wasn't going to be anything. Despite their words, I was able to graduate from high school, college, and then graduate school. So much for a person who was destined to be another statistic.

So, instead of believing the lie that I would not amount to anything, I have now replaced it with the truth that I can do anything I put my mind to. I now realize that we were all put on this earth with a purpose.

Unfortunately, many people will try to derail you from your purpose if you let them and this is why it's important to ALWAYS ask yourself, "Who are they that I should believe what they say about me? Who are they that they know the path God has set for me?"

Upon asking these questions, remind yourself of your TRUTHS. The demon of self-hate will work hard to make you forget your TRUTHS so that you are enslaved by the words and opinions of others. For this reason, I suggest that you take some time to write down all of the things that you know are true about you.

V. OWN YOUR TRUTHS. "I'm fine just the way I am." What a positive statement. Many experts and all of the self-help books recommend that you speak positive words of affirmation to yourself on a daily basis. But what they fail to inform you is that you must

truly believe the words in order for the process to work. I can say, "I love me," and "I
am the best thing since sliced bread." But
if my mind believes, "I'm a failure", or "no
one is ever going to love me," then my practice of daily words of affirmation is in vain.
Remember...you're UNIQUE, ImPERFECT,
and DIVINELY made.

VI. CHANGE YOUR SURROUNDINGS.
Whenever you're progressing in life, it may
be necessary for you to change the makeup
of your inner circle – removing people who
deplete you, while adding people that enhance or bring you joy. This may be one of
the most difficult things you will have to do
on your journey – for no one in your life is
off limits. If you find that it's your parents,
family member(s), or best friend that is depleting you (causing you distress, making you
unhappy or making you feel bad about yourself) then you MUST, in love, let them go, if
only for a season.

EXERCISES I used on my journey:

I. TRUTHS VS BELIEFS. If someone walked
up to me and said, "you're not black," or

"you're not a woman," or "your eyes are blue," I would argue them down with such conviction they would quickly be "persuaded" to change their opinion. I know for a fact that I'm black, a woman and my eyes aren't blue, and therefore confident in challenging their opinions. Hmmmm... What if I was this confident about my self-image? I would never allow anyone to speak negatively about my personality, character or physical appearance without experiencing the wrath of my sarcastic mouth. Before I could develop this type of confidence, I had to first realize MY TRUTHS. Under the advisement of my therapist, I made a list of my truths, which included but wasn't limited to:

- I'm a woman (I thought I would start with an easy one)
- I'm creative (it took me a long time to accept this)
- I'm intelligent
- I'm emotional (for years I thought this was a character flaw, but now I realize that it's a part of who I am and it makes me unique, not flawed)
- I'm an introvert (this is not to be confused with a social misfit)

- I'm 5ft 1 inch (I can add an extra inch or two with heels, but I will NEVER be the height of a model, nor do I wish to be)
- I'm loyal (I'm a woman of my word and would go to the end of the earth for those I care about)
- I'm beautiful inside and out (please don't get this confused with society's definition of beauty. For me, the more I exude inner beauty, the more beautiful I become on the outside.)
- I'm organized and structured, which could sometimes be mistaken as being OCD, (people can either take or leave it – this is who I am)
- I'm personable

I think you get the picture. I can go on and on with my truths, which is refreshing. There once was a time when I didn't know myself and wasn't able to write one thing that wasn't based on the words and thoughts of others.

While listing my truths, I was introduced to the person that died years ago. With every negative word, rejection and disappointment, Lashana died and in her place emerged a confused, scared, self-loathing little girl. In time, that little girl became an adult who allowed the demons of her past to dictate the woman she had become – a woman whose smile masked the pain she felt on the inside. No longer is this the case. I now know and accept my TRUTHS and no one can take this from me.

II. JOURNALING. If you don't enjoy writing, journaling may seem like a daunting task. However, if you journal with intent, it's easier to do. You can do it the traditional way with good ol' pen and paper, you can blog, or use a note taking app to document the events/people who make you feel inspired, motivated, happy as well as those that make you feel unhappy, not enough, depressed and depleted. While journaling, don't analyze or edit your thoughts – just write or type. Revisit your journal entries monthly and adjust your surroundings, mindset, etc. accordingly. If you find a person or event in the "positive zone," find ways to keep them in your life; if in the "negative zone," remove them as quickly as you can.

III. MIRROR, MIRROR. Change the way you look in the mirror. Instead of critiquing yourself – pointing out what you consider flaws – appreciate your ImPerfections. When I first did this exercise, I focused on my physical imperfections (my flat butt, my short legs, the moles on my face, etc.). But for as many imperfections I noticed, I had to find just as many things I appreciated about myself. So in response to my flat butt, I told myself it's the right size for my frame and it provided the right amount of cushion on hard surfaces. My short legs have definition and muscle tone, which is kind of sexy, and the moles on my face compliment my big smile. You get the point. Now you try.

IV. FORGIVENESS. Forgive those who have shaped your negative beliefs of yourself. Once I realized that people usually impart their insecurities on others, I understood that their negative words/actions were less about me and more about their own issues. With this mindset, I found myself feeling empathy for those who wronged me. Anyone who feels the need to put down someone to make themselves feel good is miserable. Aw, they may need to receive a copy of this book (smiles). Remember, forgiveness isn't for them. It's for you, so you can move on to fully embrace your truths.

Through these exercises – replacing negative beliefs with my truths, journaling, forgiving the people who destroyed my self-image etc. – I've transformed from Lashana, the mean and anti-social person to Lashana, the caring, sensitive introvert. I was introduced to the person who God intended me to be. She is neither mean nor unsocial, but is a sensitive and emotional person who is afraid of getting hurt. She is an introvert who NEEDS alone time in order to recharge. Her necessary retreat doesn't make her mean, but gives her the energy to smile, and the resources to be a blessing to others.

PART II
THE JOURNEY TO
SELF-WORTH

*No one can make you feel inferior without
your permission*

ELEANOR ROOSEVELT

CHAPTER 7

THE JOURNEY
CONTINUES

The journey to rebuild my self-image took five months, countless tears, and ten plus exhausting therapy sessions. Although I entered into therapy kicking and screaming, after my walk down memory lane, I felt like a new woman after doing the work. I replaced the beliefs I'd formed from the negative words of others with my truths – based on the person God designed me to be. A breakthrough in every sense of the word, but our work was far from over.

So at my allotted day and time, I met with my therapist for yet another session. After our pleasantries, she didn't waste any time with the difficult questions. "So tell me about the man you're currently dating. I believe you mentioned he's your neighbor."

I so wished she didn't go there. The unhealthy relationship with my neighbor was difficult to talk about. I was embarrassed to admit that I was in a relationship with a man who sort of had a girlfriend and who only spent time with me on Monday, Tuesday and Thursday nights. Only at night...classic signs of a booty call.

I repeated the question to myself and began to fidget in my seat. I felt like the room was closing in on me. I cleared my throat several times and took several sips of water.

Although not subtle, my therapist sensed my discomfort with the topic and allowed me to dance around the details about my relationship for a few minutes. I talked about how we had a good time when we were together. I lied to her and myself when I said I was too busy to be in a committed relationship, so our arrangement worked perfectly for me. Ladies, you know that if we're really digging someone, we'll carve out all the time in the world. I went on with my "song and dance" for what seemed to be ten minutes before my therapist went in for the kill with her next question. She proceeded to ask, "You're obviously not completely happy with this arrangement. Why don't you just leave?"

Leave – what an interesting concept. I thought about my answer a few moments longer. I considered lying, but then thought it best to tell the truth for my healing. And this was the moment the tears started flowing. My answer was one that breaks my heart to this day. As I wiped my tear stained face, I responded in a cracked voice, "I can't leave because I can't get anyone better than him. He's handsome, smart, funny, and successful and makes time for me when he can. I'm not pretty, smart or sexy enough for anyone to really want to be with me."

"WOW!" I'm not sure if she verbally said it, or if the expression on her face said it all. Nevertheless, I knew she couldn't quite comprehend how the woman who sat before her believed she couldn't do any better than to share a man with whom she had to barter for his time, affection, and attention. I can only assume this was when she realized the root of my low self-worth went deeper than the relationship with my neighbor.

She then asked me to tell her about the men in my past, and for some reason, without hesitation, I started talking about my father or the lack thereof. Before I knew it, I was discussing the details from my past and current relationships in which I was physically, verbally and emotionally abused. It wasn't until this conversation that I recognized the root of my low self-worth. This discussion was deep…

CHAPTER 8

DADDY'S LITTLE GIRL

I was a very confused child – looking for attention and love in all the wrong places. I grew up without a father, which I believe made me yearn for affection from the opposite sex. I'm a firm believer that a girl needs her father or some other positive male role model. He should be the example of the type of man she should date. He should teach her how to be a lady in a world where women are degraded in videos, television, music etc., and he should treat her like a princess/queen so she would never allow anyone to treat her any less. Unfortunately, my father taught me that love hurts and men leave.

Whether the birth of a child is planned or is one of life's pleasant surprises, the child is an inactive participant in this decision. A child doesn't have a choice on who its parents will be or what type of life they will have upon their entrance into the world. This wasn't any different for me when I was forced into the world kicking and screaming. If given a choice, would I have chosen to be born at a different time, if at all? Would I have chosen to be born without a father?

At various stages in my life, the answer to these questions may have been different. Today, I believe that no matter the circumstance, my birth was a blessing. However, I also know that the absence of my father or any positive male figure severely impacted my life.

Although I didn't know his name or even what he looked like – wouldn't recognize him if he passed me in the street – there always seemed to be something missing in my life. It's like knowing that you NEED something, but you're not really sure what it is. You just know without it, you're incomplete.

As a child, there was a hole in my heart that needed to be filled. Unfortunately, this need became so prevalent that I wanted it from anyone and in any way I could get it.

Before I was in the first grade, I remember trying to discover my father's identity. I asked question after question, day after day. I don't know whether my mother's answer was the result of being worn down from my questioning or her playing a joke at my expense, but whatever the reason, when she said my father was the man singing on the song playing in the background, I believed her. I needed to believe her.

"Isn't She Lovely?" was blasting from the speakers, so based on what my mother said, my father was Stevie Wonder. Upon hearing this, the hollowness in my heart was removed. My father was Stevie Wonder, the famous musician and songwriter. He didn't abandon me. He was just busy on tour and making albums, but he spoke to me through his songs – or so I believed at the time. Today, I laugh at the thought that I actually believed Stevie Wonder was my father, but I was a child in need of a father.

Every night, after learning my "father's" identity, I played his album, got on my rocking horse, and sang with the music as loud as I could. Playing his albums made him real to me. I was able to feel his presence without him actually being there. For a brief moment in my life, I was complete. I was happy and I was loved.

I don't remember how long my mother allowed me to be disillusioned, but I know at some point, she told me the truth. The devastation of the truth was almost unbearable. As soon as she said, "Stevie Wonder isn't really your father," I was overwhelmed with sadness. The hole in my heart returned and I was no longer complete. One day, I had a famous father who loved me enough to sing to me on his albums. The next day I was without a father, filled with the image of a man denying my birth and abandoning me before I was even born. I was devastated.

A girl usually idolizes her father. He's the man she looks up to, the man she compares her boyfriends to, and the man that will always hold a special place in her heart. This wasn't the case for me; I had no one to set the standard, so I went for anyone. I looked for the love I needed from my father in my relationships with boys and eventually men.

I had a boyfriend since I was in the fifth grade. I was too young to have been thinking about boys in this manner, but I yearned for their attention. This is where it all started; where I found myself relinquishing my power – doing whatever I thought was needed to keep a boy/man in my life.

In elementary school, this may have included allowing him to "feel me up" on the back of the bus or on the staircase. It also included my recurring forgiveness of him breaking up with me for some stupid reason – he started liking another girl in the class or it was Tuesday – whatever the excuse. This was the time in my life when I should have been having fun playing in the schoolyard or learning my reading, writing, and arithmetic – not worrying about why some boy didn't like me.

As you can imagine, this became progressively worse as I got older. I graduated from a "feel" to sex. Neither was acceptable, but of the two, a "feel" was safer and a lot less intrusive. It's sad to say that I've engaged in most of my sexual encounters because I thought it was something I HAD to do and not something I WANTED to do. During each encounter, I was overwhelmed with guilt and sadness. With each touch, each kiss and each stroke, the tears would flow from my eyes like a waterfall. I often felt like Celie in the movie *The Color Purple*, "he just climbs on top of me and does his business." I tried to imagine being someplace else, so I could get through it without having an emotional breakdown.

I started having sex at the young age of thirteen, as you will soon read about. If only my father played an active role in my life, he could have taught me that love isn't something you earn. Love isn't something you obtain if you do this or that. Love is an emotion felt by another, merely because of who you are, not what you do for them.

CHAPTER 9

BOOMERANG: SEAN

I became interested in boys at a young age. It was as if I wasn't complete unless a boy validated my worth. As I got older, my need for their validation grew into the need for their approval and affection.

I was only thirteen, only in the last half of the eighth grade, but I was in love with Sean, one of the most popular boys in the neighborhood. When he first asked to be my boyfriend, I remember thinking, "WOW, I can't believe Sean chose me to be his girlfriend. Why me?" Who knew that his request to be my boyfriend and my "yes" would be the beginning of a long ride on an emotional rollercoaster?

Sean was not the most attractive boy in the neighborhood, but what he lacked in looks, he made up for with his swag. He had a quiet disposition, which gave him an air of mystery. But anyone who confused his quietness for him being a punk was sadly mistaken. When a fight broke out, he spoke with his fist. He was all action, no talk, which made him the "quiet storm."

I, on the other hand, wasn't popular, was quiet – because I was trying to be someone else and thought everything I said was stupid – and my wardrobe didn't compare to some of the more fashionable girls in the neighborhood. Hence, I couldn't believe it when Sean asked me to be his girlfriend.

The minute I said "yes," my thoughts were consumed with what I would say, how I should act, or what I should wear, so I wouldn't seem so boring to him. I never knew what to wear for my clothes no longer appealed to me. I felt as if my wardrobe was an embarrassment to his reputation. Getting dressed for school in the morning was a chore, doing nothing for my confidence back then. My clothes looked frumpy to me and my reflection in the mirror looked stupid – not the image of the girl who was supposed to be Sean's girlfriend.

When I wasn't obsessing about my outfits, my thoughts were consumed with thinking about our time together. Now that we were a couple, what the hell were we supposed to do? What did popular people talk about? Would he still want to be my boyfriend once he found out that unlike him, I couldn't come and go as I pleased? I had a curfew. I had to ask permission to go off of the block, and on the weekdays I had to be in the house when the streetlights came on. It wouldn't take him long to realize I was just a lame, shy, frumpy girl who didn't deserve to be his girlfriend.

My anxiety about being Sean's girlfriend was more or less self-imposed. For as much as I was worried about what to say, dress and do around him, he was just as nervous. At times, it was as if he was more nervous than I was. This was until that unforgettable day when our relationship changed forever.

In the beginning of our relationship, we talked on the phone for hours. Now that I think about it, we probably did more listening to each other breathing or watching television than actually talking. He would stop by my house, sometimes on a daily basis, to make sure I was okay and didn't need anything. And every day when I got off the bus after school, I could count on him to be waiting for me, usually with one of his boys. My affection for Sean grew stronger every day. I felt like Sandy in the movie *Grease*, right before Danny started acting like an ass.

Although things between Sean and I were going quite well, every day I wondered if this was the day he would come to his senses and break up with me. I defined myself as "Sean's Girlfriend." This was who I was and without him I would be nothing. Therefore I would have done anything to make him happy. I was desperate to keep him in my life. Almost twenty years later and it's still hard for me to admit I completely lost myself in my efforts to retain my title as "Sean's Girlfriend."

Although I was smart (based on my grades) and was considered a cute girl (based on the comments of others), I thought I had nothing to offer in order to compete with the other girls in the neighborhood. Once again, the demon of self-hate took residence in my mind. It convinced me that I was not as cute or as cool as other girls. The war in my mind stripped me of my self-worth. What a dark place life is when you don't value yourself.

Disillusioned, I convinced myself that the only way I was going to keep Sean in my life was to give him all of me. He had my mind and soul, so the only thing left was to give him my body. I assessed the pros and cons of going all the way with Sean. This was a wasted exercise, because at the end of the day, the only thing that mattered was that I earned Sean's love. Once the decision was made, I only had to make the necessary arrangements to make it all happen. When I told Sean that I was ready to go all the way, he first asked if I was sure this was something I really wanted to do. Once I said, "yes," Sean's eyes widened, and I believe I saw all thirty-two of his teeth. One of the biggest smiles I've ever seen outside of my own.

We planned to meet up on Wednesday after school at 5pm at his house. I would tell my mother I was going to my girlfriend's house who lived around the corner. Not technically a lie. I did quickly stop by her house to say, "hi" on my way to meet Sean. My love for him clouded my judgment, but also made the obvious invisible – at the age of thirteen, I was too young to be thinking about or having sex. But this was the only way I could keep Sean as my boyfriend – or so the demon of self-hate would have me believe.

Since it was my first time, I regrettably relied on television and my friends as my "expert sex advisors." Experts they were not. If they were any kind of authority on sex, they would have educated me on the importance of having sex when both you and your partner are mature enough to embrace the true essence of this type of intimacy; waiting to have sex with someone you love and loves you as well. More importantly, they should have strongly advised me not to use sex as a measure of my love for another when I didn't love myself. Wow, if my "advisors" had shared this with me prior to my having sex with Sean, I would have thought more about my feelings for myself instead of focusing on how to make Sean love me.

In preparation for my first time with Sean, I made sure all of the important parts were fresh. I also changed into a matching pair of underwear – something I learned from watching movies. Although I saw couples having sex in movies, I was unaware of what was about to happen, which increased my nervousness, causing the pit of my stomach to ball up in knots. I walked the five blocks to his house, dreaming about how it would feel, how much more he would love me, and how strong our relationship would be after we had sex.

I arrived at his house at 5pm on the dot. Nervous, I rang the doorbell and Sean answered immediately, as if he was waiting at the door for me. Although we'd dated for several months, our greeting was awkward and almost uncomfortable. Time stood still for what seemed like an eternity and it was as if we were meeting each other for the first time.

As I remember it, we were both nervous. He was trying to play it cool, as to not let on that although not a virgin, his experience was very limited – not allowing him to develop a technique or a rhythm of his own. My nervousness came from the same place that brought me there – I was more worried about pleasing him than I was about the actual act itself. Although this was my first time, my fantasies about that day made it feel as if we were intimate several times before. In my fantasies, I experienced pleasure that brought me to a total state of bliss and uncontrollable passion that would strengthen our relationship, creating a bond between us that could never be broken.

As he escorted me to his room, I contemplated whether I was making the right decision, but unless I wanted to lose him forever, I had to go through with it. There was no turning back now.

The entire "event" lasted less than FIVE minutes, but the consequences seemed to last forever. After having sex with Sean, I realized not only did I lose my virginity, but I lost control of my emotions. Prior to our five minutes of intimacy, I was sarcastic, sometimes sassy, and was able to exude a little confidence around Sean. Not even a second after it was over, I felt all of my power being released from my body. I was no longer in control of my mind, body or soul.

During sex, it's said that you and your partner become one. There's a release of hormones that makes one feel like they are on a natural high. In addition to the release of hormones, which could be described as feeling like you've taken a "happy pill," there's also an emotional connection that transpires between one or both parties. This emotional connection is where I found myself falling into the abyss of vulnerability, low self-esteem, and lack of self-worth.

My need to be loved was intertwined with my fear of abandonment, which made for a dangerous combination. Sean became my world. It was as if I couldn't live or breathe without him. Unfortunately, Sean became acutely aware of this and began to change the way he treated me.

Prior to my "first time" with Sean, we would talk on the phone until one of us fell asleep. He would slip money into my pockets so I could shop on Jamaica Ave. And if I called him, whether on the phone or if I hollered down the street, he would come to my house without hesitation. But after our afternoon of intimacy, when I gave Sean my body, in addition to my mind and soul, things changed for the worse.

In the days that followed, Sean didn't have time to talk on the phone anymore. His friends, playing basketball, and hanging out on the block became more of a priority than our relationship. He no longer accompanied me on my walk home from school. And the pair of sneakers he bought for me "just because" was the last gift I ever received from him.

Since I was his girlfriend and it was my "duty" to have sex with him, my first time with Sean was definitely not my last. Although I never really enjoyed it – every time I had sex with him I wondered what the women on TV were moaning and groaning about – I endured sex with him because I truly believed that this was the only way I could keep him. After all, he was my world and without him I would die.

Little did I know, every time I had sex with Sean, I relinquished my power. With every lustful moment, I lost more and more of myself. I never addressed Sean's change in behavior, nor did I break up with him after he checked out of our relationship. My willingness to stay in the relationship while he did less than the bare minimum allowed him to further his abusive actions, thus stripping me of any self-worth, self-confidence or self-love I ever had.

To make matters worse, Sean started messing with other women, knowing that I would find out and selfishly knowing that I would never leave him. Our neighborhood spanned several blocks, but it was very small when it came to gossip. Although I wasn't allowed to hang out like many of my friends, I was informed of every move Sean made and every girl he flirted, spent time, or had sex with. Sean was aware of how gossip traveled within our neighborhood, but did nothing to stop the information from getting back to me. Why should he? I wasn't going anywhere. If only I knew back then that as a female, I possessed great power, my relationship with Sean would have been totally different.

Allowing him to treat me like an old toy and disrespect me by openly dating other women added to his arrogance. And my reluctance to leave him left me in a state of hopelessness. My hopelessness grew into despair when Sean added verbal and physical abuse to his treatment towards me. What once was a modern day Romeo and Juliet became more like being in a relationship with Dr. Jekyll and Mr. Hyde.

There were days when I was reminded of the first month we started going together – to use the term we used back in the day. He was sweet, kind and loving. If only every day could have been like that. Unfortunately, those days were far and few between. Most days, he was yelling at me to get out of his face, asking me why I always wanted to be around him, and making jokes about me to his boys like, "Damn she's like a stray dog that keeps coming around. Maybe I should stop feeding her and she will go away."

Being disrespected behind closed doors was bad enough, but when he allowed his boys to get a front row seat to his abuse, I wanted nothing more than to be invisible. When his boys were around, it was as if he was putting on a show. He popped me on the mouth if I spoke out of turn, repeatedly telling me to shut up and calling me stupid when I was allowed to speak. There were also times when he demanded that I stay in his room while he entertained his friends, both male and female. I did as I was told to avoid a breakup or getting smacked. I couldn't bear either one. I would sit in his room by myself, watching television, holding back tears.

After his "performances," I was stripped of my pride and on the verge of tears. I dared not to cry in front of him or his boys, for that would mean more jokes made at my expense. So I wore the mask of a smile, like a silly little schoolgirl, whenever Sean publically disrespected me. It wasn't until my short walks home that I allowed myself to cry. I couldn't let my mother or aunt see me cry. I would never have heard the end of it. If I became too emotional to go home, I would stop by a girlfriend's house to cool off. These visits were more to vent, or most often, to convince me that I wasn't a fool for staying with Sean.

My girlfriends weren't strangers to abusive boys. Unfortunately, this was the "in" thing in my neighborhood at that time. It wasn't uncommon to see a girl arguing with her boyfriend, a couple fist fighting in the street, or a guy disrespecting a girl in front of a crowd. It's sad to say that we were so misguided that we believed the more abusive the relationship, the more your boyfriend loved you. Our rationale was, he wouldn't take the time to fight with you if he didn't care about you. As I think back at this time, I shake my head in disbelief. Were we so in need of love that we convinced ourselves that abuse equated to love?

My conversations with my girlfriends would go something like this…

Me: "Girl, Sean is bugging out. He had the nerve to tell me to get out of his face and leave him the hell alone."

My Girlfriend: "Shana, you know that boy loves you. He makes sure everyone knows that you're his girl and they dare not to mess with you. He only acts like that to hide his feelings for you. He's gotta rep to protect."

Me: (with a big Kool-aid smile on my face) "I guess you're right."

My Girlfriend: "Everyone knows that you're wifey, so don't pay him no mind when he tries to impress his boys."

Me: "Yeah, I know I'm trippin'. He'll be calling me later tonight to make sure I'm home and tell me he's sorry."

My Girlfriend: "Feel better now?"

Me: (with a smile on my face) "Yeah, I'm good. So what's up with you and your man?"

Although at the time, my girlfriend and I truly believed Sean's actions were his way of showing me his love, I now realize that his treatment towards me was neither love, nor affection, but a case of ABUSE. There were times when we would be having fun – watching TV, talking on the stoop, or just walking to the store and something or nothing would trigger his barrage of insults – "You're stupid. You always want to be around me. Why can't you just leave me alone? You need to get a life, etc." Needless to say, my self-esteem diminished with every word and somewhere near the end of our relationship, my self-worth went from "on sale" to FREE.

The longer I remained in this relationship, the more it appeared as if Sean was doing everything he could to make sure I was powerless – stripped of any ounce of self-dignity I had. Two years into our relationship, I felt as if I was living in the movie *Sleeping with the Enemy*. If I made the mistake of doing, wearing, or saying the wrong thing – which was easy with my sarcastic mouth – my delicate face was greeted with his open hand.

When it came to my relationship with Sean, I tried to remember the good times –the first six months – and block out the bad. However, there was one incident I remember as if it were yesterday...

It was a nice Saturday afternoon in May. One of those days when it wasn't too hot or humid and the sun was at just the right intensity. It was the perfect day to go for a walk around the neighborhood. With no specific destination in mind, I decided to stop by Sean's house to say hello. As I walked the five or so blocks to his house, I envisioned him being happy to see me, and thought about us spending the afternoon together. This vision put a smile on my face. I was both happy and nervous at the same time. I couldn't wait to get to his house.

With a huge smile on my face, I walked around to the side door. But before I was able to raise my hand to knock on the door, he pushed it open and came out followed by a girl I vaguely remembered from school. Upon seeing her, my smile quickly turned upside down and I felt the blood rise from my feet all the way to the top of my head. Within ten seconds of seeing her, I was HOT.

The looks on their faces indicated they weren't expecting to see me when they opened the door. I guess the feeling was mutual. I was able to get out a "hello" to break the ice. Based on their delayed responses, I assumed I was intruding. I didn't know if I should walk away, or stay there and stand my ground. Unfortunately, I was frozen in place. My legs felt like blocks of cement, so I was unable to move. As I stood there, I thought to myself, "nothing good can come of this." I envisioned an argument and maybe some cursing and crying, but never in my wildest dreams was I prepared for what came next.

Once they got over their initial shock, they were both able to muster up a dry ass, "hello." They then proceeded to act like I was invisible as they hugged and said their goodbyes. A look of disbelief and anger came over my face. My blood was boiling and my anger was uncontrollable. At that moment, all logic escaped me. It was as if I was having an outer body experience. I raised my voice and shouted at the top of my lungs, "Who is she? What is she doing here?" I didn't give him a chance to reply before I started in on my next set of questions, "WTF, is she your girl-friend now?"

Sean diffused the situation by telling me to calm down. "You're my girl – you know that. She's just a friend." He then told the girl, "Let me take care of this. I'll see you around in school next week."

I foolishly thought he was professing his commit-ment to our relationship. I thought by him saying I was his girl in front of her that I was his one and only. When the words rolled off his tongue, you couldn't tell me anything. I thought I had finally won his heart. Little did I know, the two of them were fool-ing around behind my back. She had a boyfriend and wasn't looking for anything serious, so it worked out perfectly for the two of them. Not so much for me.

As she disappeared down the block, I moved to-wards the open door with such confidence thinking to myself, "Yeah, how dare that girl come between me and my man?" I walked up the five steps that led to the door, and was almost inside when I felt a hard push leaving me off balance and stumbling down the stairs. When I got my bearings, he slapped me in the face and shouted, "I hate you."

The stun of the blow shook me to my core. In just one quick moment, I was rendered powerless – stripped of whatever self-dignity and self-worth I ever had. And if that wasn't bad enough, his brother's friends were in the kitchen and witnessed the whole thing. This was all I could bear. I was embarrassed, angry and wanted nothing more than to be invisible. This blow to the face, and the many blows that followed, gave birth to the insecure, powerless, and worthless Lashana that has taken me years to rebuild. I wanted to be invisible so that no one could see my eyes fill up with tears. I wanted to be stronger so instead of standing there like a wounded puppy, I could tell Sean to forget he ever knew me and walk away forever. I wanted to love myself more so that I could end the relationship and never look back.

Unfortunately, I wasn't given the ability to be invisible and didn't have the strength to walk away or the courage to end the relationship. Instead I was defenseless – devoid of options. I needed Sean in my life, for I didn't know who I was without him. I believed this with every fiber of my being, and for this reason the only thing I could do at that time was to produce a fake half smile and walk to his room like nothing happened. I believed and wanted with all of my heart for Sean to come to his senses, and everything would be as they were when we first started dating – before we had sex.

Sean and I stayed together for three years – breaking up to make up, and me losing myself with every day that went by. To those that knew us, it seemed as if Sean and I were one of those "ghetto fairytales;" where we would beat the odds of societal constraints and work through our dysfunctional relationship, have children and live happily ever after. However, my reality was nothing like a storybook and it seemed as if I would remain on the emotional rollercoaster forever. That was until one terrifying night.

Sean and I were going through one of many breakups, so I decided it would be a good idea to put on my best outfit and attend a party that was going on around the way. I wasn't really into parties, but this night I thought it would be a good idea to get out and shake my tail feathers a little. And maybe, just maybe, Sean would be there and I could make him jealous. Thinking back on it now, this was such a recipe for disaster.

Back in the day, house parties were held in the basement. This basement was crowded and all the popular people from the neighborhood were there. As my girlfriend and I maneuvered our way down the stairs and zigzagged our way to the dance floor, I immediately found my groove and started dancing to the songs the DJ was spinning on the turntables – LL Cool J, Rakeem & Eric B just to name a few. The party was FRESH. While shaking my little tail feathers,

I thought to myself, "I'm so glad I got out of the house." That was until I caught a glimpse of Sean. At the mere sight of him, my heart started racing, my body started trembling, and I could no longer find my groove.

Unable to compose myself enough to do the basic two-step, I decided to chit-chat with my girlfriend who came with me. We talked about what people were wearing and laughed at some people's lack of rhythm. Just then, I caught a glimpse of Sean moving towards us in a very deliberate manner, as if he had an important mission to address on my side of the room. Sean didn't seem happy to see me. The look on his face made me nervous and I immediately thought twice about my decision to attend the party. I was so naive to think that my being at the party would bring him back to his senses and he would fall in love with me all over again. As I stared into Sean's eyes, I noticed that the look on his face wasn't a look of undying love, but anger – pure evil.

I was suddenly presented with a vision of Sean slapping me in the face in front of everyone in the party and I was scared. I told my friend that I was ready to go because my feet hurt. The reality was that I needed to get as far away from Sean as I could. Damn, I wished I had stayed my ass in the house. I could have been watching television in my pajamas, but instead I'm bobbing and weaving, running out of a party so I wouldn't get slapped – or worse, punched in the mouth.

When my girlfriend and I made it out the house, I breathed a sigh of relief. I was able to leave the party without incident. I was filled with a false sense of calm and didn't see any reason to rush home. So instead of taking the short way back to my house, we decided to stroll the block, talking, cracking jokes and giggling as we slowly walked the ten, long blocks home. We were having so much fun, we were totally oblivious to Sean running towards us until it was too late. As soon as I realized he was coming straight at me, Sean grabbed me by the neck, slammed me down on the trunk of a car, and proceeded to choke me with such force that I stopped breathing. The last thought I had was that of Sean killing me.

Cautiously, bystanders tried to get him off of me, but they were also fearful that he would turn his wrath on them. It took two guys and what seemed like an eternity, but they were finally able to get Sean off of me. A minute longer and I may not have been around to tell this story.

After this incident, there was no turning back. His attempt to end my life was my "wake up call." The love we once shared was gone and so was our relationship – or so I thought.

The influence the demon of self-hate had over me was strong, and my love for self was nonexistent.

Even after Sean tried to choke the life out of me, I sadly believed his act of violence was his way of expressing his love for me. I believed I would never find someone who loved me as much as Sean, so I quickly forgave him before he started dating someone else. This had to be one of the lowest points in my life – the day I decided to remain in a relationship with someone who tried to kill me.

Months following the unfortunate incident, Sean was on his best behavior. He apologized for what he did every chance he got and promised to never let his temper get the best of him – at least not until the next time he tried to kill me. Sean professed his love for me daily, spent time with me, and even started to walk me home from the bus stop. Isn't this characteristic of most abusers?

He was so nice and appeared to be genuinely sorry for what he did. I needed him to love me. I thought this time was going to be different and maybe some good would come out of the incident. I wish I could go back in time and shake some sense into my younger self. Unless they undergo therapy, an abuser will always revert back to his/ her natural tendency to OPPRESS and ABUSE the ones they care about, and Sean wasn't any different.

It only took three months before Sean forgot all about his promise to never hurt me again. I thought things were bad between us before the incident. I couldn't imagine things getting worse – but they did.

Sean regressed back to his old ways – cheating, lying, hanging out with the boys neglecting me, and of course, the frequent blows to the face. This time he added imprisonment to his arsenal of abuse. Imprisonment…you're probably envisioning all sorts of horrific things. I don't think it was anything as bad as what you're thinking, but as a teenager, what he started doing was like me being in prison.

"Sean, can I go across the bridge (those of you who are from South Jamaica, Queens know what I'm talking about) or can I go to such and such house?" This was the "permission process" I had to go through in order to go anyplace aside from my house, school or work. If Sean found out, or even suspected, that I went somewhere without permission, I would be subjected to a few slaps, a barrage of insults and his latest tactic at the time – destroying my jewelry. He knew that I didn't go anywhere without my earrings (door knockers, bamboo, the bigger the better) and chains (rope, name plate etc.). I was in hell and wasn't strong enough to escape.

This went on for months until that one summer night when once again, Sean's love for me became life-threatening…

On that unforgettable summer day, Sean must have been in a good mood because he granted me

permission to hang out with one of my girlfriends –
my road dog at the time. I told him we were going to
hang out at her house, but truly I had no clue what
was on the agenda for that day. I felt as if I was given
a day pass from prison and I was going to take full
advantage of the privilege.

With my "get out of jail free" card, my girlfriend
and I decided to go hang out in Baisley buildings,
some twenty blocks away from my house. We wanted
to have some fun and we were well aware of all the
action that took place in the buildings – boys hanging out on the corners, girls fighting for some trivial
reason and the air of excitement in places where ille-
gal activities were common. The excitement! I'm so
glad God was watching over me because my lust for
excitement could have ended me up in the hospital,
jail or dead. They say God takes care of fools and
babies, well, He sure took care of me.

After spending hours walking to the buildings,
hanging out on the playgrounds and visiting people,
we were exhausted. We couldn't bear to think about
walking back home, so we went to the nearest cab
stand – only those from certain parts of New York
know what I'm talking about – hopped in a cab and
made our way home.

During the cab ride home, we relived the day all
over again. We talked about the gossip we heard and
what boys tried to talk to us. I felt real giddy. I'd met

new people, caught the interest of several cute boys and more importantly, I was happy to have gone a full day without obsessing over Sean.

As the cab turned onto my block, I could think of nothing else but hopping in my bed and replaying the day in my dreams. Unfortunately, my plans were short-lived, because Sean had other plans for the rest of my night.

As soon as I got out of the cab, I saw Sean running down the street with gun in hand, pointed straight at the car. At the time, I didn't know if he was just trying to scare me or if he was really going to use it. Either way, I didn't want to stand there and find out. I tried to run, but didn't have enough speed to run to my house, get out my keys, and unlock the door. So instead, I stopped in my tracks and stood still with my heart beating out of my chest. It took every ounce of self-control I had not to pee on myself. My life flashed before my eyes. Did Sean finally lose it? Was I going to lose my life five feet from my house?

The next thing I remember was Sean's friend shouting, "Man, don't do it. Put the gun down." My girlfriend belted out an earth-shattering scream of fear. I would have thought all of the commotion would have enticed one of my nosey neighbors to come outside or even look out their windows, but no such luck that night. It was just the four of us on my dimly lit street with my fate in the hand of my jealous, abusive boyfriend.

With his gun pointed straight at me, Sean asked me a series of questions. "Where were you? Who were you with? What boys did you talk to?" My mind immediately went into survival mode, because I knew the wrong answer would have sent him over the edge.

I don't know if it was the adrenaline or my will to survive that gave me an overwhelming sense of calm, but I was able to answer every one of Sean's questions without crying or giving him any indication that I was being less than truthful. He must have been satisfied with my answers because he lowered the gun and put it in his waist. He then instructed me to go in the house, but not before smacking me in the face. It's sad to say, but that time I welcomed the slap. I preferred the sting of his open hand to that of a bullet.

When I was safely in my house with the door locked, I was able to unleash all of the emotion I withheld in front of Sean. I cried uncontrollably for hours. I was mad, sad, scared, frustrated and most of all disappointed in myself for allowing things to go this far. Why didn't I love myself enough to end my relationship with Sean when he tried to take my life months ago? I was weak and powerless, but I knew I had to break up with Sean. My life depended on it.

I would love to end this chapter with some heroic gesture like telling Sean off, regaining my self-worth and making him regret the day he lost me forever. But instead, this chapter of my journey ends with me finding the strength to stay away from Sean by getting involved with a boy who was crazier than Sean and would not hesitate to retaliate if Sean ever put his hands on me again. Fortunately, I only needed his protection for a short time – two to three months – until I left for college. College helped me get away from Sean, but it also allowed the demon of self-hate to further attack me, and its attack was relentless.

Telling my therapist the story about my first love was bittersweet. After all we went through, he still holds a special place in my heart to this day. But reliving the dark periods of our relationship – the abuse – was emotionally draining and I didn't have the energy to discuss yet another relationship. All I wanted to do was go home, get something to eat, and have a glass of wine. I'm not sure if our time was up. Even if the clock told a different story, my standing and gathering my belongings said, "It's time to end our session for the week."

My therapist was well aware of how emotionally draining that was for me, so she didn't try to convince me to stay a minute longer. She thanked me for sharing and gave me a hug. That was one of the few sessions that I was able to leave her office without some type of "homework."

As I walked to my car, I was tired, but I felt a little lighter. There was something liberating about sharing the details of my first love. But equally, there was also an underlying sadness in identifying the actual chain of events that altered my romantic relationship with men.

For years after that relationship, I engaged in several short (less than a year) relationships that only helped to further my lack of self-worth. With every relationship, I found myself with men who cheated or were just getting out of a relationship (code for they're still sleeping with their ex); men who just wanted to go with the flow (code for, I have no intentions of taking this any further); or men who claimed they weren't ready for a relationship (code for, if you allow me to "get the milk for free," I will).

At my next session, I walked into my therapist's office lighter and excited to move forward along my journey to healing. I assumed reliving my relationship with Sean was the most difficult. I naively thought uncovering the impact of my other two relationships were going to be a walk in the park because the worst was over. I was so wrong.

As soon as I started to retell the story of my relationship with Mark, it became evident that each of my past relationships was equally as difficult to relive, but for different reasons. When his name – *Mark* – rolled off my tongue, I was immediately showered with feelings of hurt, pain and sadness. I quickly grabbed the box of tissues. And after a deep sigh, I prepared myself for yet another emotional session…

CHAPTER 10
LOVE JONES: MARK

A few years after my relationship with Sean, I learned how to guard my heart – never allowing myself to fall that deep in love again. If only I realized that it wasn't my love for a man that was the problem. It was my inability to love myself that was the real issue. Therefore, all of my efforts were in vain. Although I was never truly in love with any of the men I dated after Sean, with every relationship, I still found myself powerless – desperately seeking love and affection from any man and in any way I could get it.

In college, I was in several different relationships, but the outcome was always the same. I would sabotage the relationship with my NEED to always want to be with them, triggered by my fear of abandonment;

my NEED for their acceptance, triggered by my lack of self-confidence; and my NEED for them to complete me, triggered by my diminished self-worth and self-image. I will now admit that I expected the impossible from several of the men in my past, for the only person that can complete me is me.

Tired of the parade of failed relationships, I decided to remove myself from the dating scene. Upon graduating from college, I focused all my energy on my career and paying the bills. That was until I met Mark.

I was introduced to Mark at a surprise birthday party for one of my college friends. Mark was handsome in an Omar Epps kind of way. He had a certain sexual appeal that made him intriguing to women, but he wouldn't necessarily be the object of every woman's fantasy. Before the party really got started, my girlfriends gave me the low down on all of the eligible men who were invited to the party. Number one on the list was Mark, so I knew where he hung out, worked, and lived before he even walked through the door. To this day, my girlfriends claim they weren't trying to set me up (wink, wink), but they wanted me to be ready, just in case.

It could have been the alcohol or the lack of single people in the room, but Mark and I instantly connected. It was apparent in the way we flirted with one another and the way we communicated on the dance floor. After four or five songs, I knew I was attracted to him – so much so that I thought to my-self, "He's all right. I could see us together." Ugh, we women are notorious for meeting a dude and within ten minutes of great conversation, we're already en-visioning ourselves walking down the aisle.

Maybe a week later, Mark and I went on our first date and not long after that, we officially became a couple. I thought I was on cloud nine. I was finally in a relationship with a man who genuinely cared about me – at least for a brief moment.

In the beginning of our relationship, it was very difficult for me to let my guard down. After Sean, I vowed never to be hurt like that again and so I put my heart in a fortress, making it hard for any man to get in. This put a slight strain on our relationship, which resulted in a great deal of frustration and un-necessary arguments. My heart was protected for so long that it was no longer a matter of me not wanting to let someone in. It was as if I didn't know how.

Mark was very patient with me and fortunately we were able to work through this issue. His willingness to fight for our relationship ignited a desire within me to do whatever it took to keep him in my life. I was so used to men walking away at the first sign of difficulty that I was overcome with admiration. I wanted to share everything with Mark – my mind, body and soul. Oh, here I go again.

The fortress that once secured my heart was gone and I was vulnerable once again. Every now and again, my mind would wander back to my relationship with Sean, but I was able to quickly remove those thoughts from my mind because with Mark, everything was different – or so I thought.

I'm not quite sure of the exact timeline, but I do remember that our GOOD relationship became BAD really fast. A little before our one-year anniversary, Mark lost his job, which didn't make him a "happy camper." I was still working hard to maintain our relationship and Mark was doing everything he could to destroy it.

On the day of our one-year anniversary, I wanted to do something special. I knew he was having a hard time with his unemployment and financial status, so I wanted to have an evening where he didn't have to worry about anything. I wanted him to smile like he did when we first met.

I planned a wonderful evening for him at my apartment. I cooked a five-course meal with all of his favorite dishes – fried chicken, macaroni and cheese, string beans, yams and cornbread. Yes, I can cook when I want to (in my sassy voice with my hand on my hip). I lit candles all around the apartment for romantic ambiance and I even had soft music playing in the background. I also had the bathroom ready for his warm, bubble bath. I was so excited, I couldn't wait to open the door and see his face.

When the doorbell rang, I leaped across the living room to open the door. When I opened the door, I jumped in his arms, giving him a BIG hug and kiss. I was like a little kid who was going to meet Santa Claus for the first time. So you can imagine the heartache I felt when Mark unfolded my arms from around his neck and gently placed my little feet on the floor. I thought to myself, maybe he's having a bad day. Once he sees what I planned for us, he'll no longer be in a grumpy mood. Boy, was I wrong.

I showed Mark the blanket that was nicely placed on the floor for us to have a candlelight dinner. He wasn't impressed. I saw the look on his face and immediately focused his attention on the food. Although he was hungry and accepted my offer for a plate, he was not half as excited as I thought he would be. After all of the planning and preparation, he sat on the couch, turned on the TV, and ate his food without saying one word to me. I was devastated. It took everything I had not to throw the plate in his face. But I didn't. Instead, I sat down and watched TV with him in silence.

After about thirty minutes, I proceeded to put away the food and clean the kitchen, defusing my disappointment and anger by keeping busy. With a clean kitchen and the television in the living room occupied by my rude boyfriend, I went into my room to calm my nerves.

Not even ten minutes later, he entered my room and gave me the look – the "I know I'm gonna get some" look. Although he wasn't in a very talkative mood, he still had the urge to have sex. Go figure. So reluctantly, I had sex with him. After all, it was part of my "girlfriend duties." I thought once we had sex, his mood would change, but after he came, he rolled over and didn't speak to me for the rest of the evening. What was supposed to be a nice romantic evening turned out to be a disaster and unfortunately, this was just the first of many BAD days.

Mark's anger with his employment situation magnified every day he was unable to find a job. Mark couldn't direct his anger at "the man" who he blamed for all of the problems in his life, so he took his anger out on me. Nothing I did or said was good enough. He would tell me all the time that I wasn't pretty enough – "Why don't you look more like Nia Long?" I wasn't thin enough – "You don't have kids so you have no excuse for your stomach not being flat." I didn't cater to him enough, and I didn't initiate sex enough. But no matter how mean he was to me, I woke up every day with one mission in life...to make Mark happy.

The more I tried to make Mark happy, the more miserable I became. Mark's constant verbal attacks and lack of affection destroyed my self-worth and eliminated any self-esteem I had. The demon of self-hate was knocking at the door and it wasn't long before it was able to assume permanent residence in my life once again. Mark made the demon's entrance easy, because he soon added cheating to the mix. I was again rendered powerless, depressed, and felt like there was no way out. I found myself rationalizing why I had to stay with Mark. It wasn't as if I could do any better. I wasn't fly, cute or thin enough to get anyone else. So I had to stay with Mark. The demon of self-hate messed me up.

I would often tell myself Mark was a good man. If he got a job, things would go back to the way they were in the beginning. It's amazing how I justified his abuse by saying, "It's not him. His situation is making him do it."

I can admit that during college, I put on a couple of extra pounds. Standing at five feet, it wasn't a good look for me to be approaching 150 pounds, wearing a size 9/10 jeans. Despite the extra weight, I wasn't obese, nor would anyone consider me overweight. Mark saw things differently and used any and every opportunity to make a big deal of my weight. He compared me to his ex-girlfriends, showing me pictures and pointing out their petite frames. He also threw in a couple of comments like, "You should have a six pack like her," pointing to a picture of his ex-girlfriend; or "you would look cute, you know, like Halle Berry, if you lost weight."

My self-image was shattered. I never thought I was drop dead gorgeous, but I would have put me in the cute category. That was until Mark. Every time he asked, "Why don't you get your hair done like other women? Why don't you go to the gym?" or any other random insult that came out of his mouth, I started to see myself in a different light. The cute girl I used to see in the mirror was replaced with a fat, frumpy girl who wanted nothing more than to be someone else. I was never going to be as pretty as Nia Long or as sexy as Halle Berry. When I looked in the mirror, I was disgusted. I hated the sight of my reflection, for all I saw was UGLY.

Two years into the relationship and I didn't know how much more I could take. Remaining in the relationship meant constant verbal abuse, but leaving meant I would have to start all over again. Who would want a fat, frumpy young woman who obviously didn't know how to make a man happy?

I allowed the demon of self-hate to influence my decisions. Hence, I remained in the relationship for what seemed like an eternity. Things continued to get progressively worse. I became numb to his words. I tuned him out just like one would do the radio when they hear a song they don't like. I was in a state a depression and became withdrawn. I no longer had the desire to kiss, touch or even be intimate with Mark.

Every time Mark touched my body, I cringed. I resorted to quick pecks on the cheek, because the thought of kissing him made me nauseous. And intimacy became more of a chore than anything else. Many times, I would cry or pretend I wasn't there.

Why did I stay? I've asked myself this question several times. Sadly, I was at such a low point in my life that I was disillusioned, thinking I couldn't get any better than Mark. I was on a path of self-destruction and I was too far gone to find the strength to turn back.

My world was like a black hole. I continued to fall deeper and deeper into the abyss until I experienced a life-altering event that gave me the courage and strength I needed to eventually end this abusive relationship.

Growing up, I always knew there was a higher power watching over me, but I didn't really give it too much thought. I went about my business and lived life according to how I thought I should live. I didn't understand or embrace the power of God until I went through a near death experience – one that changed my life forever.

It was a stormy Sunday evening, Mother's Day 2000. Mark asked me to accompany him and his mother to a dinner at his friend's house. I was excited and elated. I remember thinking that this invitation signified a turning point in our relationship. No more was I *just* another girlfriend. This invitation meant I was *the* girlfriend.

I got the call inviting me to dinner around 4pm, which only gave me a little over an hour to get dressed. I looked in my closet as if it were my first time, unimpressed with the clothes that were neatly hanging on the plastic hangers. I tried on all of my good outfits. When I look at the pictures from back in the day, I can't believe I ever walked out the house wearing some of those outfits. None of my clothes seemed to fit right that day or were appropriate for the occasion.

After almost an hour of trying on clothes and discarding them in a pile on the floor, I was now pressed for time. I only had thirty minutes to get showered, dressed and do something to my hair. I contemplated calling him and cancelling, but they were already en route to pick me up and I didn't want to be an inconvenience. Perspiration dripped from my forehead as I rushed to get dressed – not in the outfit I'd envisioned, but I looked decent.

Mark was in front of my building promptly at 5:30pm, which was great because if he were late, I would have been furious that I ran around like a chicken without a head, sweating out my perm, when I could have taken my time.

Once I got to the car, he gave me a hug and his mother offered a warm hello. With no time to spare, we quickly began our journey to New Jersey to his best friend's house. We were no more than five minutes into the ride when the car felt like it was swerving off the road. There were only a few people whose driving abilities I trusted, and Mark was not one of them. My fear was heightened by the inclement weather. It had been raining all day, so the roads were flooded, which made for dangerous driving conditions. Needless to say, when the car slid in and out of the lane, I immediately panicked and scolded him for not paying attention while driving.

At this time, I thought it was a good idea to close my eyes partially to get a quick nap, but more so I wouldn't be a back seat driver. As soon as I closed my eyes, I felt the car slipping and sliding off the road. It didn't take long for me to realize that something wasn't right. The car slowly slid four lanes from the far left all the way over to the far right lane. I guess even in terrifying situations, I'm still analytical, because while this was all taking place, I looked to see if there was any oncoming traffic – trying to assess how severe the accident was going to be. I also reviewed our surroundings to ensure there weren't any large trees we could crash into.

In the blink of an eye, I felt the car begin to tilt over, and in that moment, I saw the image of my deceased Nana saying to me, "Don't worry, my child. You're not going to die. It's not your time."

It was at that moment that a strange calm came over me. As the car tumbled over once, twice, and then three times, I knew my Nana sent the angels to protect me. I may have suffered a few bumps and bruises, but my Nana assured me it wasn't my time and I believed her.

When the car finally stopped moving, we found ourselves upside down with the car resting on its roof. Anyone else in the same situation would have panicked, but I smiled. I smiled at the thought of my Nana – a feisty woman in her day – organizing the angels to help save her grandchild.

I took a brief moment to thank God and thank my Nana, then I went into survival mode. We all took a mental survey to make sure we didn't have any severe injuries, and aside from a throbbing pain in my right hand and bruising from the seat belts, we were all fine. We were alive. Luckily, I was able to climb out of the rear window and yell for help.

Within thirty minutes, the police and paramedics arrived at the scene of the accident. We were taken to the nearest hospital for a thorough checkup. This was when I learned that I had broken a bone in my right hand that would require several weeks of therapy to heal. I didn't really comprehend all of the information the doctors were throwing at me. All I knew was that we were ALIVE.

Over the next several weeks, I suffered through my physical therapy sessions. It was the most frustrating and humbling experience of my life. For ten weeks, I was unable to write, shave my legs or tie my shoes. I was at the mercy of others to help me with trivial things I took for granted before the accident – wiping myself after I used the bathroom, doing my hair, paying my bills.

I thought I was going to therapy to fix my hand; unbeknownst to me this experience also healed my heart. As I strengthened my hand, my confidence strengthened. As I increased the mobility in my fingers, I increased my self-esteem and as I regained the power in my hand, I regained the power that I gave Mark. And although I will never have full use of my hand, my self-esteem was (briefly) restored and the demon of self-hate was temporarily evicted from my life.

At the end of my physical therapy, I was a new woman. I started eating healthier and going to the gym. I lost over thirty-five pounds. I found a beautician who I started going to on a consistent basis. A chick was looking good. I also enrolled in a graduate program to help further my career.

I was feeling really good about myself. Before the accident, I looked in the mirror and saw an ugly duckling – a woman no one wanted to be with. After therapy and a few weeks in the gym, I looked in the mirror and saw an attractive young lady who was ready to conquer the world. For the first time in a long time, I felt good about who I was. That was until I would meet with Mark.

Even after all the changes I made to my image, he still had nothing nice to say. I realized that in order to truly be happy, I would have to find the courage to end the relationship, but I didn't know how. A part of me knew that breaking up with Mark was the right thing to do. But there was another part of me – the insecure part – that tried to convince me that what I was experiencing was a temporary phase. And that once it was over, I would regret my decision to let Mark go.

I didn't know what to do, so I did nothing. I continued to bear the label and the responsibility of being his girlfriend, but I no longer felt the emotional connection that usually came with the title. It was as if I was waiting for Mark to get tired of our loveless relationship and move on – but this never happened.

Once again, it took divine intervention to help me end yet another abusive relationship. This time, God moved me to Long Island which was almost two hours away from where Mark lived. This distance made me geographically undesirable and ultimately we grew apart. It was almost six months before the relationship completely ended; but thankfully it did without either one of us having to say the words, "It's over."

The end of this relationship marked the birth of a new and improved Lashana. I was confident, strong and wasn't going to allow another man strip me of my power. I thought I defeated the demon of self-hate forever. That was until I met Steve.

Before I discussed my most recent unhealthy relationship, I decided to talk about my relationships after Mark and before I moved to Georgia. I wasn't quite ready to talk about Steve. I wished I could have avoided the topic all together, but when it came to my therapist, I knew better.

After my breakup with Mark, I needed a distraction to help ease the loneliness that came with entering singlehood after being in a three-year relationship. It didn't take me long to find someone to occupy my time. I wasn't looking for another relationship. I was looking for someone to feed my ego – someone to help me heal the wounds from years of hearing that I wasn't enough. Seek and ye shall find. And I definitely found someone who stroked my ego, at least for a short moment.

His name was Malik and he was one of those "fine for no reason" type of brothers like Boris Kodjoe. I thought I was lucky that he would even want to spend time with me. He worked security at my job at the time. He worked nights and I worked my usual 9 to 5. Our schedules made it difficult, but not impossible, for us to spend a lot of quality time together. Or at least this was the reason he fed me whenever I requested we spend more time together.

Still in awe that he gave me the time of day, I settled for short walks throughout the city, stolen glances of him as he manned the front entrance, and one (yes one) dinner date, oh yeah and one "roll in the hay." We really didn't have anything in common and our worlds and intellectual capacity were so different that we didn't have much to talk about. To be honest, he was as intelligent as a bag of rocks.

OMG, if only I knew then what I know now, I would have made him pay me for my time. I guess it's true what they say – hindsight is 20/20. As expected, the affair was short lived, but it ended not a minute too soon, because after Malik dismissed me like last year's Jordans, I started spending time with Mike, a fellow classmate in my MBA program.

He was handsome, intelligent and had just the right amount of swag. He was also in the process of breaking up with his girlfriend – code for "I'm only saying this to help ease your conscience. I have no intentions of leaving my girlfriend."

I found myself falling for this dude, hard. I truly believed he was breaking up with his girlfriend. I fantasized about the day he and I would be a couple. But as the days turned into weeks, and the weeks turned into months, my fantasy was replaced with the reality that our relationship would never be more than what it was. He didn't have any intention of ending the relationship with his girlfriend, and he damn sure wasn't going to commit to me. The heartache was more than I could bear – falling for a man who would never be more than a grad school fling.

Graduation was my "savior." It was after graduation that I was able to put distance between us to try to heal my wounded heart. I say try, because this was harder than I realized. Therefore my true "savior" was my move down south. Over 900 miles between he and I was just the distance I needed to get over Mike. Unbeknownst to me, I was running from a bad situation to find myself in yet another abusive relationship – out of the frying pan and into the fire.

Less than one year after my move from NY, I was swept off my feet by a fine, six foot one chocolate brother whose intelligence matched his looks. I fell so fast that I wasn't able to catch myself before I found myself in yet another unhealthy relationship. For five long years, I was on an emotional roller coaster that brought me to my breaking point – the relationship that led me to my darkest days. So I guess it's time I talk about this relationship. I guess it's time to talk about Steve…

CHAPTER 11
HE'S JUST NOT THAT INTO YOU: STEVE

In the time between my breakup with Mark and my next life altering relationship, I received my MBA, passed the CPA exam, moved to Atlanta, nurtured my spirituality and progressively moved up the corporate ladder. With each accomplishment, I thought I overcame my battle with the demon of self-hate. Once again, I was sadly mistaken. It's true that demons know the areas you struggle with, and through deception and confusion, they steal your joy. I thought the relationships with Sean and Mark were my all-time low. These relationships were a walk in the park compared to my next tumultuous relationship.

At the age of thirty-three, I had come to respect my singleness, almost to the point of planning for my life alone with my dog (or dogs). Maybe I would focus on my career – climbing the corporate ladder, investing my money wisely and retiring early in order to travel around the world. The more and more I planned for a life of singleness, the more the idea of being married and having kids became less appealing. Yes, I was able to convince myself that I would be happy with not having someone to share my life with, not having children and never having someone to love.

Although my mind was convinced that singleness was an ideal state for me, my heart refused to buy into this. Day after day, as my mind and my heart warred over the fate of my marital status, I continued to seek opportunities to meet new people. While I ran my weekly errands – going to Kroger's, Target and the local gas station – I couldn't help but wonder, would this be the day I meet my king? Although I didn't know when or where my king would emerge, I was well aware that he would not just knock on my door.

Therefore, you must understand my surprise when the one person I thought would be my king "knocked on my door" through an invitation to a community event. The invitation was not created professionally. It was more of a collage of words and clip art, which piqued my interest. What grown person would create such a juvenile document?

The day of the event snuck up on me. I contemplated whether I should stay in the house and relax, or go to the event and be social. After much deliberation, I decided to put on my good jeans and make my way to the event. As I approached the door to the clubhouse, I wondered if I should turn around. But before I could talk myself out of it, the doors opened and I was greeted by one of the most handsome men I had laid eyes on.

Prior to this encounter, I thought love at first sight was a concept that was made for television or the movies. Never did I imagine that I would experience this mystical feeling. As our eyes locked, I remember losing myself for what seemed like five minutes and then thinking, "I have met my husband."

After the normal introductions, we found ourselves embraced in what would appear to be a friendly hug, however, due to our immediate chemistry, it was more of a seductive embrace. Being in his arms felt comfortable and familiar. I could have stayed there forever. After what seemed like an eternity, we parted – both confused and captivated by our initial embrace.

After I unglued my eyes from his handsome face, I realized that I was in a crowded room filled with my neighbors, many of whom I'd never formally met. Steve, on the other hand, knew everyone in the room by their first name and address. I must have been living under a rock, because I know I would have noticed a fine man like Steve while walking my dog, going to the mailbox, or taking out the trash.

Steve led me around the room to meet my neighbors. "I want you to meet Ron, Mike, LaToya, and Gwen."

I introduced myself, gave them a big smile, and tried to remember as many names as I could. We then walked over to the buffet table to where a young lady was helping herself to the nicely arranged appetizers. He acknowledged her and turned to me, "Lashana, meet my girlfriend, Dana."

It took me a couple of seconds to actually register what he said. How could the man of my dreams have a girlfriend? God, was this some type of joke?

After my surprise introduction to my soul-mate's girlfriend, I immediately felt the sudden urge to run out of the clubhouse and never look back. As not to be rude, I filled a small plate with some fruit, cheese and crackers – none of which I was able to eat. After playing with my food and meeting a few more people, I excused myself and went home. I needed to get in a quiet place and ask God the reason for the cruel joke. Why did He introduce me to the man of my dreams if he was unavailable?

Fortunately, Steve and I didn't run into each other for some time after the event. Although I thought about him occasionally, it was best if our paths never crossed again. I often fantasized about the day Steve would ring my doorbell and ask me out on date. This type of stuff never happens in real life and definitely not in mine. So you can imagine my surprise when I received an email (yes an email) from Steve asking me to go out to dinner.

I couldn't think of anything else during the days leading up to our date. I'd dreamed about this day several times, and now that it was a reality, I was nervous. I felt like a schoolgirl preparing for her first date. What should I wear? What do I talk about? Will we have a good time? Even though I'd gone on several dates, this was different.

Steve picked me up at my house promptly at 7pm. We didn't confirm where we would eat, but since it was my birthday weekend, Steve told me to pick the spot. My love for seafood led me to choose Pappadeaux. The first ten minutes were easy. Once we were seated, we did the normal intense study of the menu combined with a little small talk. Once we placed our order, I wondered, "Now what?" But once I allowed myself to relax, our conversation became more natural. We discussed our careers, plans for the future, and recent books we read. I wonder if he noticed my constant staring. I couldn't believe the man I'd daydreamed about for so many months was actually sitting across from me.

If the night couldn't get any better, Steve revealed his adoring side. At the end of dinner, I noticed Steve holding a piece of paper in his hand. At first, I thought it was a flyer to another event, but when he handed it to me and I read it closely, I realized it was neither a flyer, nor information about the community. What he handed me was a homemade birthday card containing the same clip art montage as the flyer for the community event. I was flattered that he took the time to create my very own personalized birthday wish. There was nothing that could take away the smile I had on my face.

Unfortunately, we had to leave the restaurant, but I didn't want the night to end. When he got to my house, he parked in the driveway where we continued our conversation from dinner. We discussed his recent break-up (you'll soon read that I should have delved a little further into this topic), vacations, marriage and various random topics. As the time neared 12am, we decided to end our wonderful evening and promised to make plans for another date.

The next couple of days were total bliss. Steve and I talked on the phone conversing about everything from neighborhood gossip to our childhoods. Some nights, we would spend hours on the phone and would only end the conversation when one of us was too tired to really hold the phone – and even then, we tried to hold out as long as we could.

Steve was very outgoing and loved to talk whereas I loved to listen, so we complemented each other perfectly. It felt great to be with someone who was handsome, intelligent, had a sense of humor, and shared many of the same interests. The more we spoke to one another, the more comfortable we became. In a short time, our conversations were less like two neighbors talking and more like a couple who knew each other for years. During our time together, we didn't focus on our past relationships since both of us were single – or so I thought. Now in hindsight, I wish I had spent more time delving into the reason why he and his ex-girlfriend broke up, or even his feelings for her.

Since we were spending a lot of time with one another, I was delusional in thinking that we were building a friendship that could potentially turn into something more. Steve did many nice things for me when we first started dating, or whatever we were doing. He knew I was writing a book, so he offered resources to help to get my book published. Yes, the very same book you're reading now. He would also check to make sure I'd eaten, knowing that cooking was not an activity I did often. He kept me abreast of important neighborhood news, knowing that I rarely read the association notices. And he invited me over to watch movies, knowing my love for movies.

In addition to all of the other things, he also went out of his way to do little things to show he cared. One evening, he had his friend who was a chef prepare dinner for me. Steve went out and purchased all of the food and made sure he stocked his fridge with Pepsi – aware that this was my soda of choice. For my dining pleasure, his friend prepared chicken lasagna, which I thoroughly enjoyed. Although he didn't do the actual cooking, I could tell Steve put a lot of thought and effort into the dinner. He cleaned the house, selected a nice mixture of R&B tunes to play in the background, and the table was romantically set just for him and I. I had such a great time that evening. I held on to that moment for a long time, because that was one of the last romantic gestures Steve ever performed for me.

As I continued to revel in our romantic evening together, our movie nights and our long talks on the phone, I was totally blindsided when I discovered Steve and his ex-girlfriend were rekindling their relationship. The worst part about it was, I found out while riding past his house one Friday evening and noticed her car in his driveway. I remembered the car from that weekend we first met and I noticed the car sitting in his driveway from time to time. This alone would not have been a red flag, but her car remained in his driveway Saturday and Sunday evenings. I was pissed.

My anger was further ignited by his blatant avoidance. During that weekend, he wouldn't respond to my texts or take any of my calls. Hell, I would have accepted an email from him just so I could calm my nerves. When she finally left his house on Monday, I called Steve once again and to my surprise, he answered.

My heart was pounding, hands were sweating and my voice suddenly became soft and shaky. After our less than warm "hellos," I wasted no time. "What's going on? Are you back with your ex-girlfriend?"

His response pissed me off. "It's complicated. We're not together, but we're working things out." I couldn't believe my ears. I wished we had the conversation face to face so I could have slapped the shit out of him. Was he serious? At that point, I didn't know what to say. My body went numb and I suddenly became tongue-tied. After several seconds of awkward silence, I asked my last question for the evening. "Do you want to get back together with her?" My heart sank when he replied, "I don't know."

The days, weeks, and months following our conversations were awkward, to say the least. Steve and I continued to talk on the phone, which didn't make the situation any easier. Every time we spoke, I had to bite my tongue, because all I wanted to talk about was his decision to officially be with his ex-girlfriend. During this time, we would also go out for a bite to eat – keeping the conversation very light, never once addressing the elephant in the room. The more time we spent together, the stronger my feelings grew for him. I knew every time we went out or spoke on the phone, I was playing with fire, but my heart wouldn't let me stop. And since it didn't seem as if he made a decision one way or the other, I believed there was hope for him and I. I so wished I would have given him his walking papers after I found out he was entertaining the thought of getting back with his ex-girlfriend. I would have saved myself five years of heartache, pain and abuse.

I tried to put my "big girl panties" on and told him we couldn't be friends. The situation was too much for me to bear and I needed time to get over him. He agreed without any hesitation. It was as if he was relieved, which shattered my already broken heart. I had to get this man out of my system before I became an emotional wreck.

Two weeks into my "big girl" stance and I was ready to give in. I missed his voice, his touch and his kiss. I could no longer hold up the boundaries I'd placed between us. I had to see him. So I called him, hoping he would have an update on his situation. He was happy to hear from me, which put a smile on my face, and shortly after our pleasantries, he invited me over to his house to watch movies. Missing him and longing for his touch, I immediately agreed. I don't know if I allowed him to finish asking the question before I said, "YES." All I remember was that I eagerly agreed and quickly got off the phone, put on my clothes, and walked to his house.

I must have run the short distance to his house, because it wasn't even ten minutes between the time we got off the phone and I rang his doorbell. Every warning sign in my body was going off, but I ignored them. My feelings for him were strong so much so that I was willing to ignore the warning signs just to spend a few hours with him. I didn't know what he had decided to do about his relationship with his ex-girlfriend and at that exact moment, I didn't care. I NEEDED him.

There was a small part of me that wanted to believe that this would be the night that helped him decide to be with me. I hoped that at some point during the evening, he would realize that this situation affected me, him, and his ex-girlfriend, and he needed to make a decision or run the risk of losing both of us. Of course, my needing him overpowered my ability to clearly articulate my thoughts. So I was only able to tell him about my frustration with the situation – as if he didn't know.

As I looked into his eyes and took pleasure in being in his arms, my sense of reason went out the window. I forgot how upset I was, and found myself thinking about nothing more than becoming one with him. As he led me by the hand to the bedroom, I remember saying to myself, "Nothing good can come of this."

Once in the bedroom, we were unable to control our physical attraction for one another. We began kissing passionately, caressing each other with light, delicate touches as our bodies touched in all the right places. R&B music played in the background as our bodies moved to the rhythm. This went on for five minutes, but because of our desire for one another, it felt like an eternity. Neither one of us was able to control ourselves. We frantically removed each other's clothes. We couldn't wait any longer.

As we lay there naked, kissing, touching and caressing, we reached our peak, and just when I thought I couldn't take it anymore, we became one. Our rhythm was slow and deliberate. I wanted this feeling to last forever, but unfortunately fate wouldn't have it. After we both climaxed, we fell into a deep sleep, cuddling and touching each other throughout the night. Waking up to that handsome man beside me after a night of passion put a smile on my face.

However, my smile quickly turned into a frown as we were awakened by his ex's daily wake-up call. And it was then I realized he didn't respect me, nor did he share the same feelings I had for him. I realized I had to end this affair or he would continue to break my heart.

I replayed the events of the previous night and wondered how could a man share a passionate night with one woman and turn around and pretend to be in a relationship with another? How could I have been so stupid? How could I have not seen the signs? He wasn't trying to work things out with his ex-girlfriend. He was just trying to fulfill his "manly needs" while he waited to see where their relationship would go. Even after the truth hit me in the face like a ton of bricks, I was still unable to give up on what we could have. If her wake-up call wasn't enough, I needed another knife in my heart in order to realize that this man was just not that into me.

I sent him a text asking if he wanted to watch the NBA playoff game with me. This was game six. He was rooting for the Lakers and I, Boston. Instead of receiving a response like "Sure, I would love to," I received a message with some lame excuse like, "I've been working hard. I'm tired. I will see." His response threw me over the edge.

Although I knew my relationship with Steve wasn't healthy, I so longed for the days in the beginning when he was attentive, wanted to spend time with me, and she was not in the picture. Until this point, I thought Steve was just going through a confusing time in his life, needing to make some difficult decisions. I didn't like the situation, but I never once questioned Steve's feelings for me until that moment. His actions at that time made me doubt that he ever liked me.

I couldn't understand why he started dating me or continued to date me once he even considered getting back with his ex-girlfriend. What hurt the most, in addition to feeling used and lied to, was I thought Steve was a caring person who above all tried to do the right thing. However, his actions were evidence to the contrary. I asked myself, how could I have been such a poor judge of character? How could I have been so stupid?

For three years, I allowed Steve to treat me like less than the queen God purposed me to be. Somewhere along the way, my love for him shaped who I was, what I felt and how I acted. In loving him, I lost myself.

Steve would pacify me by periodically showing me attention, telling me what he thought I wanted to hear. When necessary, he eluded to a time in the near future when he and I could be a couple.

If only I had loved myself more, I could have told him where to put all of his empty promises. Up and down on the rollercoaster, I endured all of the heartache and disappointment of being with a man who was incapable of truly loving anyone but himself. For a long time, I thought the void that kept us apart was his ex-girlfriend's endless pursuit to get him back, ignoring the fact that he was an active participant in all of this. He could have easily ended it – by either breaking things off with me or ending things with his ex-girlfriend once and for all.

I guess I could have also done my part to end things. This could have all been avoided if I paid attention to the movie, *He's Just Not That Into You.* If a man wants to be with you, he'll make every effort to do so – otherwise he's just making excuses.

After Steve and his ex-girlfriend parted ways, he became better at feeding my need for attention, but all the while remained non-committal. With her out of the picture, I was confident that this would be our time to be a couple. However, Steve had other plans for his newfound freedom. He avoided the topic of us becoming a couple. He would change the subject, telling me he needed time to think for months at a time. Oh and my favorite – he asked me to "go with the flow" since things between us were good. It took me longer than it should have, but I finally got the hint – Steve NEVER had any intentions of us getting together.

Once his ex-girlfriend was completely out of the picture, Steve started to show his true colors. The days of us spending time together two to three times per week were over. I was lucky to see him twice per month and that was only to have sex. Our lengthy phone conversations were replaced with only text messages. And if ever we went out to eat, it was always at the Waffle House in our neighborhood. He did everything he could to keep me at bay while doing just enough – for a person who lacked self-worth – to hold me in his web of deceit. Over the next year, Steve showed me very little attention. To make matters worse, he started dating other women – bringing them to his house for my viewing pleasure.

There were several times when I became sick and tired of how Steve treated me. I even went as far as to start dating other men. But it was as if Steve had "Spidey Senses," because just when I thought I could move on, Steve would pop back into my life, showering me with attention like he did when we first started dating four years prior. It was emotional abuse.

He was my puppet master, pulling the strings to my heart. It was as if I couldn't think for myself. I sought his opinion on everything. I was brainwashed into thinking what we had was ideal for a busy career woman like myself. Bullshit! The saddest part was that after four years of our tumultuous relationship, I believed I couldn't do any better. There must have been something wrong with me if Steve didn't want me to be his girlfriend. I was in a bad place when it came to Steve. I lost myself in this relationship and didn't know how to find me. That was until that unfortunate evening in January.

Whether it was love, my insecurity or a combination of both, when it came to Steve, I endured more than the average fool. The blatant disrespect, dishonesty and emotional torment should have been enough for me to curse his ass out, change my number and never speak to or hear from him again. Unfortunately, this was not the case. I didn't come to my senses until our relationship became so toxic that I thought we were going to be featured on an episode of *Snapped*.

I allowed Steve to steal every ounce of dignity I had. My consistent forgiveness of his indiscretions was, for him, permission to flaunt his girlfriends in my face. As with so many times before, I would get mad, threaten to never speak to him again, but in a couple of days, I would forgive him and hop right back on the emotional rollercoaster. This went on for so long, it became our new normal. This was until that unforgettable night that ended our relationship forever.

It was January 1st 2011, the day after everyone partied like it was 1999 (in my Prince voice), and I was feeling a little less than festive. For some reason, the holidays always brought on a strange sense of sadness, sometimes to the point of depression. My depression would slowly creep in right after Halloween and would miraculously dissipate February 15th. This holiday season was no different. But in addition to depression, I was also overcome by a feeling of uneasiness. Something wasn't right, but I didn't know what.

My aunt, who was in the holiday spirit that year, hosted a New Year's Eve get-together – an evening filled with good food, plenty of laughs and the best of company. It should have been easy for me to enjoy the party, but I just couldn't make myself have a good time. I tried to engage in light conversation and put on a fake smile, until I could no longer pretend. I wasn't feeling festive. Something wasn't right, and I needed to be by myself.

On the verge of tears, I left my aunt's house right after midnight and before the party really got started. I apologized to everyone for leaving the party early, giving some lame excuse that I was tired and was barely able to keep my eyes open. I wished that were truly the reason for my early departure, instead of the uneasy feeling in the pit of my stomach. I would have never imagined the chain of events that shortly transpired – the events that could have ended in a physical altercation with Steve or worse, a call to the local police, followed by a restraining order.

As I mentioned previously, Steve and I lived in close proximity, which allowed me to drive by his house without going out of my way. That's exactly what I did that night, hoping he was home alone and I could stop by for a little companionship. However, as I turned the corner, my worse fear stared me right in the face. The car of one of Steve's many admirers was parked in his driveway. So not only was he dating other women, he was spending the holidays with them. The holidays, which were typically reserved for that special someone, which obviously wasn't me. Blood immediately rushed from my feet to my head. My heart was beating so loud, it drowned the music I was playing in the car. Water flooded my eyes until I was blinded by my tears.

How could he do this to me again? Why did I allow him to think it was okay to disrespect me? My sadness was quickly replaced with anger. I was consumed with rage. It was if I was having an outer body experience. Somewhere between heartache and pain, I "snapped."

I stopped crying long enough to make the drive home. But once my garage door closed, the dam broke and I could no longer hold back my tears. I cried so hard, I could barely catch my breath. My emotions alternated between sadness and anger. Using a random tissue I found in my car, I wiped my tears and blew my nose. Steve showed me his ass for the last time and I was finally tired of his shit.

I briefly thought about going in the house and letting this blow over, as I'd done so many times in the past. However, this time was different – my rage got the best of me. My hands were shaking as I turned the steering wheel and backed out of the garage. It was impossible for me to think clearly. I was on my way to Steve's house. I didn't know what I was going to say or do, but I knew I was fed up and wasn't going to be treated like that anymore.

I don't remember parking my car or walking to his front door, but the next thing I knew, I was ringing his doorbell. To add insult to injury, as I was ringing the bell, the Chinese food delivery guy was walking up the driveway. Okay, so not only did he make the time to spend with some other chic, he also made preparations for them to have a little romantic dinner. Oh, hell no.

After what seemed like an eternity, Steve opened the door expecting to see the delivery guy. You could imagine his surprise when he was greeted by my angry face. He tried to smile as to appear cool calm and collected, but he couldn't quite convince himself – or me for that matter. This was the first time in the history of our relationship that I had the courage, or enough anger, to confront him.

He paid the delivery guy and as soon as he pulled off, I started with the finger pointing, neck rolling and the barrage of questions. "What the hell are you doing? Who is she? Why do you keep doing this to me?"

I didn't give him a chance to answer before I let him have it. "You don't deserve a woman like me. You're an egotistical asshole who only cares about himself. I can't stand your ass and I wish I never met you." I was talking so fast, he didn't get a chance to get a word in, so he took full advantage of my brief pause as I caught my breath.

He quickly went into defense mode and instead of answering my questions or being apologetic, he turned everything around on me. He had the nerve to accuse me of being disrespectful by coming to his house uninvited. He also had the audacity to inform me that I was not his girlfriend and had no right to be upset when other women came to his house. He ended his little speech by saying he was tired of me and whatever we had going on wasn't working for him. I couldn't believe my ears. Was he serious?

In that moment, I weighed my options. I could go up in his house and break up his little rendezvous or I could walk away from a man who wasn't worth my energy or the gas I wasted to get to his house. Although irrational, I chose to go up in his house. He was standing in the doorway and just when I stepped towards him to move him out of the way, he quickly slammed the door in my face and left me outside, embarrassed and pissed off.

I guess it was good that he closed the door. My mind was flooded with images of a fight, police, and a possible visit to the precinct. The lyrics in Jazmine Sullivan's song popped into my head, "I bust the windows out his car." On the short drive back to my house, I played out the events in my mind and finally came to my senses. No man is worth my freedom.

Although I calmed down, I was still a little sad and didn't want to be alone. So I did what most women do in this situation. I called one of my sistah friends, opened up a bottle of wine, and poured my heart out. After more tears and two bottles of wine, I declared that this was the last time I allowed Steve or any other man to treat me less than the queen God purposed me to be. Although this scene was not much different from in times past, I was different. I was ready to move on and I asked her to hold me accountable to make sure I didn't go back on my word. This time, I was strangely at peace with the situation. From that day forward, I vowed that Steve would cease to have the power to steal my peace, joy and happiness. From that day forward, Steve would only be yet another painful memory.

The next day I woke up with a new outlook on life – ready to live a life without Steve and excited about what the future held. This thing with

Steve must have played out in my dreams because I couldn't stop my mind from planning for my new life. By lunch, I planned to put my house on the market, sell my furniture and find residence in another county. I needed to get as far away from Steve as I could possibly get.

I must admit, I wished things had turned out differently. There were also times when I wondered if he would come to senses and we could one day be a couple. I realize this was me still trying to find good in a man who treated me like shit. I know that being with him meant I would lose every bit of peace and self-respect I had, and therefore I had no choice but to walk away. But it was hard.

By February, less than a month after the incident, my house was under contract. I sold my furniture and moved into an apartment in the city. Although drastic, I knew this was not enough to keep me away from Steve if he put his charm on me. So I changed my cell number, removed him as my friend on Facebook, and deleted all traces of his contact information from my cell phone. To this day, my interaction with Steve is nonexistent and I have completely moved on with my life. I'm in a healthy relationship and open to the possibilities of marriage. Steve still holds a special place in my heart, but to quote Beyoncé, Steve was, "the best thing I never had."

CHAPTER 12

THE PATH TO HEALING: SELF-WORTH

It took several months for me and my therapist to replenish my self-worth. Even after I shared the details of my relationships with Sean, Mark and Steve, I continued to make excuses for the way they treated me – still believing it was my fault for not being enough. With the completion of each assigned exercise, I began to value myself a little more each day.

Taking the journey through my past relationships was painful, but very therapeutic. I realized that I ALLOWED Sean, Mark, and Steve to depreciate my self-worth, destroy my self-image and diminish my self-confidence. I lost myself in each relationship, making them the center of my life – forgetting that the true center is God.

I used to beat myself up asking, "Why didn't I see the signs? How could I have been so stupid?" The truth is, I didn't want to see the signs. My need to be loved overpowered my senses – blinding me to the signs that were obviously there. It really didn't matter how bright the warning signs, I didn't love myself enough to end any of these relationships when they became abusive.

I shed many tears, endured more abuse than I care to remember, and spent a great deal of time trying to make someone love me. Unfortunately, the healing process can't begin until you're truly ready to move on. This may mean that you'll be without a "boo" for a minute and you may go through an angry phase as you assess the relationship in which you gave more than you received. There may even be a moment of weakness where you begin to convince yourself that things with him weren't that bad. If you find yourself lonely, angry or desperate, keep yourself busy, spend time with family/friends, find a hobby, and allow yourself to recall each and every time he disrespected and degraded you – not treating you like the queen you are.

INSIGHTS I learned on my journey:

I. I MUST SHOW PEOPLE HOW TO TREAT ME. I'm now a firm believer that I set the standard for how others should treat me. If

I allow, by not speaking up or addressing his behavior, a man to get away with disrespecting me once, he'll assume it's acceptable to do it again and again. Each time I allowed Sean, Mark and Steve back in my life after their blatant disrespect, indiscretions and abuse, they knew I put myself "on sale" and so did they.

II. ABUSE IS NEVER AN EXPRESSION OF LOVE. Enough said!

III. I MUST TRUST AND LISTEN TO MY "SPIRIT MAN." Some people may call this a gut feeling. Others may call it their subconscious. My therapist referred to it as my reptilian. Regardless of what you call it, it's important for me to take heed when my intuition indicates something is wrong. In my case, my spirit man was literally screaming for me to run – not walk – away from Sean, Mark, and Steve. However, my insecurities made me doubt and ignore the screams. My DESIRE to be in a relationship at all costs overshadowed my NEED to love myself. But not anymore!

IV. I ALREADY POSSESS THE POWER I SEEK. As part of my journey, I had to regain my power. It was easy for me to play the role of a victim – believing everything happened to me. It never occurred to me that I possessed the power. Things didn't happen TO ME, they happened FOR ME. This was a very hard pill to swallow. How did I have the power to make my ex-boyfriends love and respect me? Here lies the problem...I can't make someone love me. Either they do or they don't. But I have the power to walk away from a man who doesn't treat me the way I deserve to be treated. I thought if a man cheated on me, it was my fault. It never occurred to me that his cheating was his way of telling me he didn't deserve me. His loss!!!

EXERCISES I used on my journey:

I.   DESCRIBE MY KING. This exercise helped me to identify the characteristics I want in my mate. Keeping this list in the forefront made it easier for me to determine if a man was worth my time and energy. If he didn't possess eight out of the ten of these qualities, he should immediately be given his "walking papers." My king needs to be...
   • Mentally Stimulating – I don't need a nerd, but I do need someone I can engage

in stimulating conversation with about everything from movies to politics.

- Honest – The foundation of every relationship is trust. Therefore I need a man who is honest and places the same value on honesty as I do.
- A man of his word – Is it too much to ask for a man that means what he says, and says what he means?
- Loyal – He needs to be mature enough to keep it in his pants.
- God Fearing!
- Supportive – I need someone who is genuinely interested in what I'm doing, who would provide assistance if needed, who encourages me, AND who holds me accountable to the goals I establish for myself.
- Patience – I realize marriage is hard work, therefore we both will need to practice a great deal of patience.
- Selfless – A partnership can't work if one party is looking out for him/herself.
- Compassionate – Do I need to say more?
- Able to "get me" – He needs to appreciate my quirks, my flaws and imperfections.

As you can see, my list doesn't include any physical characteristics. I WANT someone who is tall, dark and handsome, but what I NEED is someone who possesses the qualities I've outlined in the list above. Oddly enough, Steve only possessed three out of ten qualities, which also helped in my decision to walk away (after five long years). He wasn't even my ideal man...so why was I wasting my time? Exactly!

II. OBSERVE THE TIMES WHEN YOU FEEL INSECURE AND THOSE INSTANCES WHERE YOU FEEL LIKE A DIAMOND. This exercise was very eye opening.

- I noticed I felt insecure when I wasn't cherished, felt abandoned, was lied to, disrespected; when my love languages (quality time & words of affirmation) weren't spoken; when I felt the person I was with was involved with someone else or when I wasn't appreciated. Hmmm, this sounds like my relationships with Sean, Mark and especially Steve, which meant I was insecure the majority of my time with these men. I don't know about you. This is not how I want to feel when I'm in a relationship.
- I noticed I felt like a diamond when... I was given attention, heard my love

languages, was able to truly be myself, or when I was shown love.

III. LIST WHAT YOUR HAPPINESS LOOKS LIKE. I must admit, I needed the help of my therapist to complete this exercise. For most of my life, I was brainwashed into believing that I should want to be married, have two children and live in a house in the suburbs. My therapist had to challenge me to think about what I truly wanted and not what society thought was appropriate. There's a reason there are so many unhappy people in traditional relationships. I believe everyone needs to assess which type of relationship is appropriate for them and enjoy. With her help, this is what I came up with:

- I want to be married, which to me means a partnership between two people where both parties have an unconditional love and respect for one another.
- Here's a big one...I decided not to have children. You should see the expression on people's faces when I tell them this. You would think I told them I was a serial killer or something. Fortunately, I have come to accept my decision not to have kids. So now when asked why I don't want

to have kids, I counter their question by asking, why do you want to have kids? There goes that sarcasm again (smile).

- Living on purpose in every area of my life. There's nothing more frustrating than engaging in activities, including your job/career, that don't bring you joy or better yet, are not aligned with your passion(s). Hence the saying, "love what you do and do what you love."

- Having a supportive and loving circle of family and friends. There will be days when the demon of self-hate will try to steal your joy. This is when you need to lean on your circle to help you defeat the demon's selfish attacks.

- Financial freedom – having the financial means to do what I enjoy, live out my purpose, and be a blessing to others. Basically, I want to enjoy the prosperity God intended for me to have.

- Peace!

IV. TELL YOUR STORY IN THE THIRD PERSON. Do you ever notice that it's easier to help someone with their problems while your life remains in shambles? I know this was (is) the case for me, which made this exercise mind blowing. I started telling my story as if it were a third party, thus taking away the personal and emotional connection. As I shared this with my girlfriends, I found myself asking, "Why doesn't this girl leave? No one is holding a gun to her head. Why doesn't she date since they're not technically together?" The more I discussed my situation in the third person, the more sick and tired I became, until I became sick and tired of being sick and tired. This was when I was finally ready to move on!

Now that I've identified what I need in a relationship/man, I'm not willing to settle for less. I also know that God can't give me His best if I continue to settle for less. No longer am I a clearance item. I now think of myself as that couture item; unique, high priced and only for a select few.

PART III
SELF-CONFIDENCE

Associate with men of good quality if you esteem your own reputation; for it is better to be alone than in bad company

GEORGE WASHINGTON

CHAPTER 13

THE JOURNEY PROGRESSES

My new value proposition – I'm worthy of God's best – peace, prosperity, passion and joy – changed my self-perception. No longer did I believe I was undeserving of love. I was ready to embrace happiness, whether it meant being single or in a healthy relationship. I AM ENOUGH!

When I walked into my therapist's office, she immediately noticed a change in my disposition. My smile was authentic. I was full of joy. I was glowing. She gave me a warm heart-filled hug, expressing her approval of my progress. I was on cloud nine. Not only was my self-esteem at an all-time high, I just knew it was going to be my last session. Although

I really liked my therapist, I was ready to get my Saturdays back. After all...I was healed. Together, we rebuilt my self-image and self-worth and for the first time in a long while, I was happy.

My therapist started our session by summarizing where I started on my journey – a broken depressed woman – to where I was that day – the happy woman she saw before her. I impatiently anticipated her next words, "You're cured. Our work here is done." But instead, she asked me how things were going with my friends and at work. I thought to myself, "Oh boy, here we go again."

I started my response as I always did – very vague, without any context. But as our conversation proceeded, I found myself saying, "My friends are great. They enhance me, although I'm not quite sure why they want to be friends with me." As soon as the words came out of my mouth, I knew I was in for another series of sessions. Damn it!

She then asked, "So what about work?" I had to think about that one for a minute, then I answered, "Work, is work. I'm not the best financial analyst, manager or leader. I'm not sure where/if I add any value." Damn, damn, damn! I just verbally signed up for at least five more sessions.

The next thing I heard was my therapist asking me, "If your friends are as great as you say, I'm sure they only associate with people who are just as great. And you once mentioned you've been promoted several times in a short time span. I'm sure your company believes you are a valuable employee. So this being the case, why don't you have confidence in what you bring to the table, both personally and professionally?"

The tears started flowing when I answered her with a sob filled, "I think it stemmed from past experiences with girlfriends, teachers and coworkers." And so the journey progresses...

CHAPTER 14

SCHOOL DAZE

Have you ever felt alone in a crowded room? If you haven't, you should consider yourself lucky, for this was the state I lived in between the ages of ten (give or take) and thirty-eight. Although not a stranger to loneliness, I never felt more alone than when I went away to college. This was when I first faced my sad reality; I didn't know who I was, and I didn't like the woman I was becoming – a woman wearing masks to hide her true self.

Teenagers go away to college to get an education and experience pseudo-adulthood while having the time of their lives. The college experience is one I don't regret, and I would encourage all teenagers who have the opportunity to go away to college to do so. From the outside looking in, my college years were not much different from any other teenager. However, the demons I faced every day made it difficult for me to truly embrace the "college experience." My weekends of partying were coupled with nights of bitter darkness. My so-called freedom was obstructed by my internal prison, and my desire to fellowship with others was complicated by my fear of being "found out."

In college, my desired outfit was jeans, a sweatshirt and a pair of matching sneakers. At the time, I probably had over fifteen pairs of sneakers in all colors of the rainbow. I thought the way I dressed signified who I was. I was comfortable with my attire and thought of myself as a confident person.

What I didn't know at the time was the confidence I thought I had was nothing more than another one of my many masks. I had a false sense confidence. The way I dressed was not a representation of my personality, but a copycat of the girls I went to school with – in a *Single White Female* kind of way. These girls were always stylish in the latest sneakers and name brand outfits to match. They exuded a certain presence that I envied. Foolishly, I thought that if I dressed like them, I could also emulate their level of confidence. Unbeknownst to me, and what I now know, is that it's not the clothes that make a person. A person's confidence and beauty is a direct reflection of what's on the inside. Self-confidence is what remains when you're stripped of your clothes, material possessions, and/or titles.

My false sense of confidence was threatened when after not even a month at college, a young man I secretly admired asked me, "Why do you wear sneakers all the time? You look and dress like a boy."

He might as well have told me that I looked like a dog, because as soon as he asked the question, I immediately felt like the Elephant Man. With just a few words, he was able to crush my spirit. Although I hid my embarrassment by repaying his insult with one of my own, it didn't change the fact that after his comment, I was no longer comfortable in my jeans and sneakers. I wanted to go back to my dorm room and throw away all of my clothes, replacing them with dresses and heels.

As I write these words, my heart aches at the thought that the only way for me to feel confident about myself was to act, dress, and talk like someone else. Forced to remove my mask and abandon the identity I'd assumed for several years, I found myself asking, "Who do I need to be? Just being me wasn't good enough. Who should I copy now?"

On a campus full of stylish, confident (based on my perception), intelligent, young women, it didn't take me long to find someone I wanted to emulate. Her name was Kim. She and I were classmates, and being two of the handful of blacks in the School of Business, we easily formed a bond. In my eyes, Kim had it going on. She was everything I wasn't and everything I wished I could have been. She always rocked the latest fashion and wasn't afraid to add her own flare to every outfit. She was able to dress up or dress down a pair of jeans and always managed to look tasteful. Her presence demanded attention and because of the way she carried herself, she was well respected on campus. Anyone would have loved to be her if only for one day. I, too, wanted to be her at any cost.

I found myself dressing like her, not like the Bobbsey Twins, but one could tell that her style influenced my new look. I also mirrored some of her mannerisms and speech. I thought by being like Kim, I would be happy. No one would know who I really was and they would all like the new Shana.

I don't have to say it, but this didn't make me happy. Trying to be someone else was frustrating. I became aggravated when I wasn't able to act and dress exactly like her. It was like being an actress in a play and forgetting my lines. To add to my frustration, I became annoyed when glimpses of my true self would emerge. I was miserable and in a state of utter despair and depression. No matter how hard I tried to disguise who I was, my true self always found a way to emerge...you are who you are.

In college, I associated with three groups of females who differed in every way from how often they partied, their popularity on campus, and family background, to the importance they placed on education. Looking back, I guess each group offered pieces of my authentic self, which may be the reason I tried so hard to be a part of each group.

THE GOOD GIRLS

When I was with the first group – let's call them "the good girls" – I was Lashana, reserved, into my studies, and more of a homebody. With this group, I was able to have fun whether at a party or just chilling in our dorm rooms. I was able to be my quirky self when it came to the way I dressed, danced, or interacted with boys. They also got my sarcastic sense of humor (much like the comedian Vince Vaughn). Despite our fun times together, we were different in so many ways, such as our family background, the way we were raised, and our values.

I was raised by a single woman in the ghetto of Queens, New York, where I was exposed to more than many of my classmates. Although none of the young ladies in this group were raised with silver spoons in their mouths, they were sheltered from the evils of the world – the drugs, abuse, and the struggles. I wasn't so lucky. I witnessed a lot (shoot outs, drug use, crimes etc.), which shaped my thinking, behavior and attitude. Because their life experiences weren't the same, I felt the need to suppress this part of me, thus wearing yet another mask.

While in college, I didn't have the luxury of calling mommy or daddy to add money to my meal card. Whatever I received from my loan check and my campus job, where I earned $30/week at best, was it for the semester, so I had to spend wisely. Whereas my friends in this group were able to make one phone call home to get financial relief for food, clothes and the occasional partying (you know, the important stuff). At times, I felt "less than" because I couldn't afford to do all of the things they were able to do. I used to make excuses like I was too tired or I had to study so I didn't have to tell them the sad truth – I couldn't afford to hang with the big girls.

As we spent more time together, I also discovered our perspectives on life, marriage, and raising children were at opposite ends of the spectrum – like night and day. I recall making the mistake of sharing my views on how much parents should do for their children. I believed there should be a healthy balance between providing for and spoiling a child. Therefore, it may be necessary for parents to practice "tough love" in order to prepare their children for the big, bad world. Giving a child everything he/ she wants could lead to entitlement, selfishness, and dependence. They looked at me as if I confessed to committing a murder. They spent an hour trying to convince me that my thinking was wrong.

This happened a few more times; I would voice my opinion and they would look at me as if I had two heads, then explain why my opinion was incorrect. After maybe the tenth time, I stopped sharing with them. At the risk of being further judged, I kept my opinions to myself. Our conversations became more superficial and I started to feel less comfortable around them. Our interactions became more like casual acquaintances – the polite "hello" as we passed each other on our way to class and maybe the occasional lunch in the cafeteria. Eventually, this became the reason for me distancing myself from this group by the end of our sophomore year.

THE HOME GIRLS

With group two, let's call them "the home girls," I was Shana – less reserved, a social drinker, partying occasionally and a little less into my studies – but still valuing the importance of an education. With this group, I had the most fun. We were like family, although we were different in so many ways. Our friendship extended beyond the campus. When we went home on break, we connected for social functions, shopping, and the occasional house parties. Although I could have completely been myself around them, the demon of self-hate never ceased to remind me that if I ever took my mask off, they wouldn't like me, just like my mother.

With the demon of self-hate in my right and left ear, I wasn't free to truly be me. So I often found myself avoiding certain topics of conversation as not to be judged. I pasted a smile on my face when we went shopping, knowing that on the inside, I was miserable. I hated going shopping in college. Every dime I had was accounted for, so there was a consequence to each purchase I made – something wasn't going to get paid or another month of ramen noodles. I know they wouldn't have cared if I never purchased one item. It was more about spending time with one another versus the actual purchases. But the demon of self-hate had me all confused. I was more consumed with being "found out" versus being myself around the one group that would have appreciated the real me.

Unfortunately, I couldn't appreciate the friendships I had within this group. It was as if my insecurities never allowed me to be completely happy, nor was I able to let anyone – especially females – truly get to know me. I was in pain, fearful of rejection, in need of validation, yearning for acceptance, and pretending to be anyone else but me.

THE PARTY GIRLS

The third group was the group with whom I felt least like myself. With this group I was Nicole – party girl, drinking five out of seven days a week, loud, and studying whenever it didn't interfere with my socializing. We shared similar backgrounds, home environments and neighborhoods, but this was where our similarities ended. I envied their friendships (they were a close knit group), their fashion sense and their popularity on campus. I wanted to be a part of this group, even if it meant losing more of myself in the process.

Every day was a party with this group and for me that was horrifying. I was comfortable with one big party a week (if that) or two house parties/get-togethers (still my preference to this day). So for me, partying every day was like being in the movie *Carrie* – a nightmare. Depending on the party, I forced myself into one of my many masks, psyched myself into having a good time, and worst of all, I had to find the courage to be social. Usually this came in the form of "liquid courage." I felt much more confident after a few drinks. Since I was a struggling college student, this meant several cups of the cheap stuff – Mad Dog 20/20, Boones Wine, and Cisco. Drinks I bet were a shock to my liver.

I did a lot of things I thought I needed to like drinking, partying etc., in order to gain the acceptance of this group. But no matter how hard I tried, I never really fit it. How could I? I was never truly myself around them, so our time together seemed forced. I was pretending to be more like them (or so I thought) and they were trying to get to know me – which was impossible given the fact that I was NEVER myself around them. Although they were never blatantly mean to me, deep down inside, I knew I wasn't really part of their group. I was merely someone they tolerated from time to time, which was devastating to my already fragile self-esteem. Needless to say, trying to a part of this group was exhausting…it was a LONG four years.

Clinically, I don't think I would have been diagnosed as schizophrenic, but my multiple personalities could have been perceived as some type of disorder. Depending on the day of the week or the group I was rolling with at the time, a person could have either interacted with Lashana, Shana or Nicole – or in rare circumstances, all three. Being three different people was difficult and frustrating at best. From day to day, or minute to minute, I didn't know who I was. And if ever I had to be in the company of people within two different groups at the same time, I was an emotional wreck.

A typical college week for me consisted of classes, socializing with one of the three groups, working and competing for the affection of one young man or another. At least four out of seven of those days, I cried myself to sleep listening to Jodeci's *Forever my Lady* (the entire tape) or Boys II Men's "Please Don't Go."

At night – alone in my bed – was my time to release the internal torment I endured trying to be someone else.

I was alone. I didn't have anyone I could talk to, nor did I have anyone to help take the pain away. So I healed myself the only way I knew how at the time – alcohol, crying myself to sleep at night, and journaling. Let's just say my four years of college were not at all the fun times people usually associate with the college life. Instead of the best four years of my life, college was more like an internal hell.

I thought graduation was the end of my internal conflict. I foolishly believed that the confidence I lacked in college would miraculously be restored the minute I got into the real world. If I knew then what I know now, I would have opted to stay an extra year and get my Masters. Maybe in that extra year or two, I would have found myself and become better pre-pared for the big, bad world I found myself forced into after graduation. The real world was no place for a young woman with low self-confidence, no self-worth and a diminished self-image. Unfortunately, I had to learn this the hard way.

CHAPTER 15
SEX AND THE CITY

As I watched one of my favorite chic flicks, *Sex and the City*, I was overcome with emotion; thinking about the support and love four women (Carrie, Samantha, Maranda, and Charlotte) had for one another. Amidst all of the relationship drama with Big and Aidan, and all of the fashion, there was an underlying story about four friends who would go through any lengths to protect one another. It's sad to think that this is the type of friendship many women long for, but may never experience.

I can just imagine all of my male readers rolling their eyes and wondering if they should continue reading or skip to the next chapter. I assure you that this chapter isn't a critique of a chick flick, but the beginning of my journey to finding sisterhood while finding myself.

It wasn't easy for me to develop long lasting friendships – the kind depicted in *Sex and the City*. Unfortunately, I had to experience a great deal of betrayal, heartache and disappointment before meeting the group of women who today I call my sistah friends. Because of the reoccurring backstabbing and jealousy, I distrusted everyone who crossed my path – especially women. In my experience, women were the worst.

My first best friend was the daughter of one of my mother's friends. We were born a month apart and to further solidify our fated friendship, we shared the same name, with only a "d" differentiating our names, Lashana and LaShanda. We were destined to be best friends forever – or in this case, until we reached high school. From birth, we were inseparable – sleepovers every weekend, dressing alike and sharing our most intimate secrets. It was as if we were sisters, which is one of the reasons I was devastated when she betrayed me, ending our friendship forever.

We went to different schools, and lived in different neighborhoods, but we spent most weekends together. Since her grandparents were strict, LaShanda spent most of her summers at my house. Like I said, we were like sisters. The summer before I entered the eleventh grade, LaShanda stayed at my house as she had so many times in the past. That summer was the busiest of my teenage years. I worked two jobs, prepared for college, (PSAT) and tried to maintain a social life. LaShanda also had a job. It was part-time and less demanding than either of my jobs. Therefore, she had a lot of free time on her hands.

Even as a teenager, I saved for a "rainy day." Every two weeks, I cashed my paychecks, put most in the bank, and put the rest in my "stash," which was an envelope tucked away in the top of my closet between my sweaters. The only one who knew where I kept my stash was LaShanda. As my best friend, I thought I could trust her with my life. Little did I know, I should have kept a close eye on her and my money.

That summer, Sean and I were going through one of our "off" periods. So during that time, I took a liking to Craig, one of the neighborhood's popular "pharmaceutical distributors," if you know what I mean. I knew him for years, but that summer, something about him changed. He grew into his big head, started working out, and wore the freshest clothes. He was like a caterpillar that transformed into a beautiful butterfly overnight. He was FINE. His new look piqued my interest – wink, wink. I flirted with Craig when I saw him around the neighborhood, which I made sure would happen at least once a day. The only one who knew about my crush was LaShanda. I wish I never trusted her with this secret.

Although my mother wasn't as strict as LaShanda's grandparents, she still had rules. These rules included cleaning the kitchen and bathroom once a week. I guess it was no coincidence that every week, LaShanda found some excuse to go home for a day or so, as to not help with the chores. Therefore, I didn't find it odd when LaShanda one day packed up all of her clothes and went home without saying a word. I was too busy to make a big deal out it, so I went on as business as usual.

What was odd was the cold shoulder Craig gave me when I walked past him the day after LaShanda left – no hug and no brief conversation. This happened two more times before I got up the nerve to find out what was going on.

Me: What's up, Craig? You've been acting kinda shady lately.
Craig: Nothing's up. You just be playing games.

At first I thought he was joking, but the expression on his face said otherwise.

Me: Whatcha talking about?

I assume he sensed that I had no clue what he was talking about, so he began to explain.

> Craig: Yo shorty, I gave your girl LaShanda a chain to give you and your ass didn't say thank you or anything. What's up with that? Then another day, I asked your girl what's up with you and she said you was just flirting with me to make Sean mad and since you two got back together, you were going to pawn the chain and leave me hanging. Your girl LaShanda be bugging. She then asked me what was up with her and I. That's some shit.

My jaw dropped. I couldn't believe what I was hearing. How could LaShanda play me like that? I assured him that I never received the chain, didn't get back together with Sean, nor did I know anything about his conversation with LaShanda. After thirty minutes of convincing, Craig and I were cool again.

As I walked the long ten blocks home, I replayed the chain of events that took place over the past five days, and it was then I realized LaShanda's abrupt departure had nothing to do with chores. As the thought hit me, I started to pick up the pace. My stroll turned into a jog. I couldn't wait to get home to call LaShanda and curse her out.

Before I called her, something told me to take inventory of my stuff to see if anything else was missing. I checked my clothes. There were two shirts missing, but I convinced myself that she put them in her bag by mistake. Then I checked my rainy day fund. My heart stopped when I found the empty envelope – the $500 I'd saved was gone. She took all of it. I was HOT!

I tried calling LaShanda several times, but kept getting her answering machine. I was so hot, I called her grandparents, but that was a waste of time because in their eyes, LaShanda could do no wrong. They've since learned that she was a devil in disguise, but at that time, she was still their little angel.

I couldn't believe LaShanda would steal from me – first my chain, my boy crush and then my money. This was my first, but not my last, lesson on the betrayal of girlfriends. That was the summer LaShanda was considered dead to me and the summer I vowed never to have a best friend.

After the demise of my friendship with LaShanda and the combination of my experiences in college, I was all but through with having female friends. After college, I had maybe four girlfriends, including my cousin, who I could call if I needed to, but life – relocation, marriage, kids – made it difficult for us to remain close. Therefore, for years, I was never really close to anyone – forced to share my thoughts, secrets and dreams with myself...I was alone. My solitude made it easy for the demon of self-hate to consume me. It made me believe that I wasn't worthy of true friendship, for who would want to be my friend anyway? I wasn't enough. Thank God for eventually sending me a fabulous group of women who helped me remove this belief.

May 2002, I moved from New York to Atlanta with only a dollar and a dream in pursuit of a better quality of life. I was disillusioned into believing that the perfect job, house, and car were enough to make me happy. I was naive to think material things could compensate for the bouts of loneliness I was going to endure from being in a new state without friends or a significant other. I didn't intend to go back to school, wasn't a member of a church, and didn't have a job just yet, so where else did one find and develop friendships?

I spent the first few weeks in Atlanta surrounded by my family, day in and day out. This was safe for me. The mere thought of meeting new people was scary. What if they didn't like me once they got to know me, or what if they betrayed me? As not to become a hermit, I went out occasionally with acquaintances I met through my aunt and cousin.

On the surface, acquaintances were enough. What did I really have to offer a friend? I didn't have a full time job so funds were low. I didn't have much going on because I was new to the city and I was different from everyone else, or at least I thought so.

The week I mailed out what my bank account deemed as my last car payment, I was offered a position at one of the top companies in Atlanta. I was finally on my way to the life I envisioned many months ago when I decided to move south. My new job not only helped to restore my confidence (again, here goes that false sense of confidence), it provided me with the funds I needed to start enjoying life. Enjoying life was a little difficult as a loner.

My cousin, April, the one person who has been with me through thick and thin, introduced me to several nice women. However, I was apprehensive about getting too close for fear of being rejected. I was plagued with memories of my teenage years when I was betrayed by my friend since birth, and my years in college, when I tried to unsuccessfully fit into three different groups.

I survived the spring and summer months by being a chameleon – living behind a mask. I tried my best to be a social person – going out every weekend, never passing up the opportunity to attend a social event and never allowing myself to get close to anyone. The more I wore the masks, the more miserable I became.

Who was I fooling? I wasn't a social butterfly. I didn't mind going to a club every once in a while to dance and listen to good music, but I preferred to spend my weekends going to dinner and the movies. However, to most people, dinner and a movie didn't count as fun. Only lame people had fun eating and watching movies, and who wanted to be friends with a lame person? So I wore the mask of a social butterfly much longer than I would have liked. And as in times past, the demon of self-hate was able to make an unwanted appearance.

The demon of self-hate was slowly making its way into my life. The longer it stayed, the harder it was for me to cultivate friendships or even feel comfortable around people. I longed to have friends who I trusted and with whom I could truly be myself. This is where the demon of self-hate crippled me as it had so many times in the past... "Be yourself. How could you do this when you don't even know who you are? And once they get to know you, they won't like you. Your own mother doesn't like you."

I was flooded with every negative word, thought, and emotion from my past. I was defeated and there was nothing more I could do but to withdraw and give up on the hope of ever having healthy friendships.

This went on for almost a year before I finally broke down and shared what I was going through with my cousin, April. She was the only person I trusted at the time, and the only person who understood my journey from where I grew up to where I was then. I felt I needed to share this with her, or else I would live the life of a little ol' maid for the rest of my life, with only my dogs to keep me company.

With every word that poured out of my mouth, I felt the release of the yoke that held me in bondage for so many years. Tears streamed down my face and I found comfort in knowing that she also struggled with this same issue. How much do you share of your past as not to be judged by the people in your present? Our lives had the makings of a black gangster movie – the drugs, number running, stolen goods, guns and crimes. Yeah, this could be a topic of a whole other book. To see us now, no one would believe our story anyway, so why share?

I would be lying if I told you that my conversation with April solved all of my issues. That would have been too easy. But it did make it more comfortable for me to at least enjoy the company of others. I needed a little divine intervention in order for me to truly allow others into my circle of trust. This was a job for God.

At the time, my emotional state was characterized by feelings of frustration, helplessness and loneliness, similar to times past when the demon of self-hate made itself an unwelcome resident in my life. However, this time, he wasn't prepared for my secret weapon – God.

Maybe a year after moving to Georgia, I started attending church. I've always had a relationship with God, especially after my devastating car accident some years before, but I never felt the need to take my personal relationship and put it on display in church. To add to this, growing up, my perception of church was that of a group of religious people gathering on Sundays to pass judgment on people who weren't just like them. Needless to say, church was the last place I wanted to spend my Sunday mornings. This was until I moved to the south where introductions went something like this...

Random Person: "What's your name?"

Me: "Lashana."

Random Person: "That's a nice name."

Me: "Thank you."

Random Person: "Where are you from?"

Me: "New York."

Random Person: "Oh, you're a northerner."

Me: (trying to contain my composure) "Yes, I'm from the north."

Random Person: "So, where's your church home?"

Me: "I don't go to church. I don't have a church home."

Random Person: (looking me up and down with judging eyes) "You need to find a church home. Everyone has to go to church on Sunday."

Me: (impatiently wanting the conversation to end) "Thank you. I'll look into that. Nice meeting you." *Not*

Random Person: "Nice meeting you, too. Let me know if you need the names of a few church homes to visit."

Me: "I will." (as I quickly walked away sucking my teeth and rolling my eyes.)

After what seemed like the hundredth time of being asked about a church home, I thought I would at least give the church thing a try. I didn't see any harm in going to church once. Who knew that one Sunday would turn into three years of Sundays? Although my perception of *most* attendees didn't change – they were still religious, judgmental people – I found myself developing a relationship with God that was stronger and deeper than anything I could have imagined. I read the Bible from cover to cover. I learned the meaning behind many of the parables, and I discovered my own way of speaking and hearing from God. It was deep. I even got baptized to seal the deal. I was all in.

Spirituality is a journey just like the one I'm taking you on. My arsenal to defeat the demon of self-hate was equipped with more weapons than ever before. The demon of self-hate found itself being attacked when it came to areas of my life that it once was able to easily penetrate, such as my financial freedom (I had a bad case of poverty mentality) and my peace. However in the areas of my self-image, self-worth and self-confidence, God was still working on me.

My firm relationship with God gave me the strength to pursue companionship – both male and female. In time, I started spending more and more time with a very interesting group of women. On the outside, it seemed we were a group of well put together women – like we had it going on.

But if you looked a little closer, we were a group of sophisticated, crazy, broken, talented woman who together would help one another survive the trials and tribulations of life. We were like family. We cared for, cried with, and even cursed at one another. No matter how angry we were at one another, we always had each other's back. And once we discovered that we were more alike than we were different, we were inseparable. These ladies became my "Sex and the City." They were my sistah friends.

Together, my sistah friends and I founded a woman's organization – SHADES (Sisters Having a Dedicated Effect on Society). We had a logo, shirts, bylaws etc. You couldn't tell us nothing. We were a group of women from diverse backgrounds and education with a passion for making an impact in the world. It was great. We met every month to plan community service events, share professional and personal experiences and network. I was pre-occupied with planning and executing our many projects, enjoying our group, and helping the com-munity. I didn't realize that demon of self-hate was busy at work, once again. Damn it!

Since my journey to healing was in its infancy, I wasn't equipped to defend myself against the feel-ings of abandonment and paranoia the demon of self-hate infected me with as I forged relationships with my sistah friends. And it was well aware of this. So it didn't hold back any punches.

One of the ladies in the group and I favored one another – so much so people mistook us for sisters. Her name was Lisa. I thought it flattering the more people would ask us if we were related; making ref-erence to our big, bright smiles, our height (we were both vertically challenged), and our facial features. I was asked so often that I started answering "yes".

My flattery soon turned into insecurity when Lisa, my play sister, said with a straight face, "We may look alike, but people can tell us apart because I dress better than you. I'm way more stylish. Whereas you're more conservative, plain, and wear no color."

I studied her face to see if she was joking, but there was no smirk, nor were her words followed by a,

"Girl, you know I'm joking." She was dead serious. At that moment, I felt like the frumpy stepsister. I found the need to defend my choice of colors and style. My thoughts instantly went back to college where I was told I dressed and looked like a boy. I thought about how hard I tried to emulate the style of others to fit in and I was HURT.

I'm quite sure her intentions were not malicious, but that didn't matter at the time. The damage was done. I was on the path of accepting who I really was and just like that, the devil of self-hate used her to cause a major setback on my journey to self-love. On the inside, I was angry with her – very angry – but I never publically expressed this until right now. Instead of talking to her about it, I decided to prove her wrong. Friends, the worst thing you can ever do is go out of your way to prove someone wrong. This strategy will backfire every time.

I spent several hundreds of dollars to add color to my wardrobe. I purchased clothes I thought would make me more fashionable. I hope you're joining me as I roll my eyes at the term "more fashionable." At some point – months after she made the comment – I asked myself, "When did she become the authority on fashion? If I felt comfortable in my clothes, who the hell was she to tell me different?" I wished I asked that question before I redid my wardrobe.

I sure proved her wrong. I wasted a lot of money on clothes that I would never wear and she still believed she was the more fashionable. I know, you're thinking, "This should have been an easy fix. Just start buying clothes you like – problem solved."

Unfortunately, the root of the problem had less to do with the actual pieces of clothing and more to do with me being comfortable in my own skin. If I accepted myself for who I was, neither she, nor anyone else could have made me feel bad about being me. I like black, brown, beige, and white and every now and again, I may throw in a splash of color. This is who I am, and it doesn't make me any more or less fashionable than anyone else. However, I didn't have this revelation years ago, so I allowed her words to shape my self-image and diminish my self-confidence.

My diminished self-confidence had me apologizing for my wardrobe choices – always being the first to reference my lack of color or my not being flashy. If I said it first, I thought I was addressing the elephant in the room, thus eliminating the jokes that would have come at my expense. The demon of self-hate had me trippin'. I was so self-conscious that I thought everyone was talking about the way I dressed. I was straight paranoid.

Getting dressed to go out with the girls was torture; nothing fit right and my clothes looked like potato sacks when I looked in the mirror. I dreaded the stares and snide remarks I *imagined* my girlfriends giving me. Of course, this was all in my head. But the demon of self-hate had me paranoid. I believed all of my girlfriends felt the same way as Lisa, and they were all talking about me behind my back. A chick was messed up!

I'd love to say my paranoia and fashion torment lasted a short while, but then I would be lying. It wasn't until recently that I began to feel comfortable in my clothes, and love the image reflecting back at me in the mirror. It wasn't until a year into my therapy that I was able to truly accept my style of dress. It's not better or worse than anyone else's style – it just is what it is.

Spending time with God helped me to get past this. Although I couldn't forget what Lisa said, I didn't allow it to ruin the friendships I had with my group of sistah friends. The incident with Lisa helped me to understand the true meaning of friendship. In the past, if something like this had happened, I would have been all in my feelings and would have distanced myself from Lisa and the other women in the group. Because of my fear of abandonment and betrayal, I would have slowly removed myself from the friendships, to guard my heart from getting hurt.

It was only through God I was able to trust the women He placed in my life; understanding He put each and every one of them in my life for a reason. Through Him, I learned that the *Sex and the City* type of friendship wasn't something you walked away from at the first sign of a problem. You pray, you fight, and you cherish this type of friendship. It's because of Him I was able to love these women as family; accepting the good with the bad. And to this day, these women are still my sistah friends.

CHAPTER 16
THE PURSUIT OF HAPPYNESS

How far can you go in your career or business if you lack self-confidence? The answer may surprise you, depending on who you ask. I believe we all have doubts within some area of our professional lives – especially women. Even the most successful woman can have insecurities in the way she walks, talks, acts and leads in relation to her male counterparts.

Many of us go to work, day after day, looking for some sort of validation from our bosses or senior leadership. If given a pat on the back, we assume a false sense of confidence – confidence that's easily crushed when we make a mistake or we don't receive an accolade we felt we deserved, or if we're passed over for a promotion, etc. If we were truly confident, our abilities couldn't be undermined by a bad day at work or a setback in our careers.

Often times, it takes someone else to highlight our accomplishments and talents before we become aware of our own value. It's like someone showing us our reflection in the mirror. When one lacks self-confidence, it's difficult for them to showcase or even share their talents or gifts with others.

A lack of self-confidence can present itself in many forms. As it relates to us professionally, it can manifest in our lack of assertiveness when speaking to people (whether in groups or one-on-one), second-guessing ourselves, never voicing our thoughts or opinions, or avoidance of leadership roles. In isolation, these issues can be characterized as being an introvert, fear of public speaking, or poor leadership skills.

Although lacking self-confidence in these areas may delay career advancement, there is a plethora of resources available to assist people who want to enhance their public speaking, communication and leadership skills. I don't want to discount anyone who lacks confidence in any one of these areas. However, in this chapter, when I talk about lack of self-confidence, I'm referring to the fear of being found out – the phenomenon that takes place in your mind when you receive a promotion or experience a major achievement and you question whether you'll be found out because you don't believe you deserve the recognition given.

At my college graduation, I remember wondering if they would find out I wasn't as smart as I appeared to be. They would realize I didn't deserve the degree, and this would be the day I would be "found out." Until my name was called and I walked across the stage, I sat in my chair experiencing a mini panic attack, not knowing if I was really going to receive my degree.

After each promotion, I waited for the day when my manager would come to me and say, "We're sorry, but after further review of your work, we don't think you deserve this promotion." Hence the reason I never celebrated a promotion until it was actually reflected in my paycheck. My theory was, once I was paid for the promotion, they wouldn't take it back. Call me crazy, but this was how I coped with my lack of self-confidence.

Instead of celebrating my accomplishments, through my lack of self-confidence, the demon of self-hate was able to diminish my light. Professionally, it was as if I was faking it until I made it. I wore the mask of a confident person every day, but the minute my work was questioned, criticized or not recognized, I had an internal pity party. This pity party would last for days during which I would doubt my ability to do the job, question whether I was in the wrong career, oh and I would always play "small" (not speaking up, being extra careful when submitting work and taking a backseat in meetings). When I was recognized for something I did well, I would downplay it and make reference to what I didn't do well to not draw attention to myself. The more attention, the quicker it was for them to find out I didn't deserve it.

My lack of self-confidence was sabotaging my career. My thinking was hindering me from reaching my fullest potential. If I didn't believe in my abilities, who would? I asked myself this question after I passed the CPA exam, graduated with my MBA, and was promoted from a temporary employee to a director within seven years. My answer made me cry. After everything I'd accomplished, I still didn't believe I did anything worth recognizing. I wasn't happy or fulfilled and I needed to know why.

Fueled by the negative words from adults like Charles and Bernard, I poured all of myself into academics and worked really hard to get good grades. With the goal of graduating from high school and college as a way to give both Charles and Bernard the middle finger. However, I must admit, school didn't come as easy to me as some thought. I had to really study and focus. And to add to the challenge, the harder I tried, the more the demon of self-hate would whisper to me, "You're not smart. They're going to find out your secret. You should give up and become the statistic you were destined to be."

In class, I wore the mask of the "good student" – the one who completed homework and extra credit assignments. But behind the closed doors of my room, I STRUGGLED. Elementary school was fairly easy in that I could comprehend the subject matter and understand the application in real life. Yes, I was that child – the one who always questioned, "Why are we learning this?" I guess some things never change. You are who you are. Middle school was a little harder, but the topics were still relatable, so although I had to study a little more than some of my classmates, I was able to eventually understand the material. This was not the case in high school.

My efforts in elementary and middle school paid off. I was able to skip ninth grade, which meant I entered high school in the tenth grade (which presented another set of challenges from a social standpoint, but that's a topic for another book). In addition, my grades automatically classified me as an honors student. Take that Charles and Bernard.

I enrolled in the local high school, which like many local schools was a combination of students who were enrolled but never went, average students (this was the group I SHOULD have been a part of), and students who were considered advanced (this was the group I was placed in). Classified as an honor student, I had to choose my area of concentration. I was offered Engineering (nope, not for me), Education (nope, I was barely able to get myself through school), math and science (an option) and a few other areas of concentrations. I chose math and science. I wanted to pursue a career in accounting, so math was a no brainer and biology was interesting, so science should have been cool. I sure wish I was given a syllabus like you get in college when you pick your major, because I definitely would have chosen differently had I known some of the extremely ridiculous and difficult classes I had to take and pass.

The subjects I was able to excel at in elementary and middle school became an academic nightmare in high school. I took Spanish in middle school, but in high school, it was conversational and focused on conjugating verbs. I was barely fluent in the English language, so needless to say, high school Spanish was challenging. Math and science became more like a foreign language. My lovely algebra was replaced with trigonometry and calculus. And biology, which initially got me interested in science, was replaced with chemistry and physics.

When I advanced to trigonometry and chemistry, achieving an "A" was impossible. I was lucky to make a "B" and that was pushing it. Chemistry to me was a cruel joke; something to make students believe they weren't smart. Trigonometry wasn't math. It was a language some genius developed to make him/herself feel smarter. What the hell was an arcsine, cosine or tangent and when in life was I ever going to use this? NEVER! And let's not even talk about physics. My teachers were dead wrong for even introducing me to the subject.

In my forty years of life, I have never used anything I learned in any of these classes. Unfortunately, in high school, passing these subjects was the only way I was going to reach "destination college" and was one of the things keeping me from proving my haters wrong. For these reasons, I had to continue wearing the masks. I had to keep up the facade of the "good student," despite the demon's consistent reminder of the words, "You're never going to be more than a statistic".

My constant academic struggle and average grades further diminished my already fragile self-image. This was the only area of my life I thought I had under control. I allowed academics to define me; I was the "good student." Raising my hand in class became a thing of the past. I barely knew my name when in class, let alone the answer to a trigonometry or chemistry question. With my lack of comprehension and falling grades, how could I keep up my façade? I would be found out and then who would I be?

For three years, tenth through twelfth grades, I "hustled" my way through high school and the rest was a little bit of luck. I leveraged the help of my classmates – a diverse group of thirty with only five black students – who seemed to be taught this stuff at birth. It's amazing how you can get the help of others just by playing to their egos. They helped me with my extra credit assignments and homework that made it possible for me to boost my C+ to a solid B. I also enrolled in classes that I enjoyed, like computers and Latin, to help with my grade point average as well as my confidence.

The other unfortunate event that helped in my graduating from high school was the early departure of the teacher that was running the math & science program. Because of her passing, I wasn't required to complete the dissertation I had to write in order to graduate.

My topic was the impact of sickle cell anemia on African Americans. I interviewed several doctors and researched the topic, but I had no clue as to how to begin this almost 20-page report I had to create. I just knew not completing my dissertation was going to be the death of me. I wasn't going to graduate and

I wouldn't be able to rub my diploma in the faces of Charles and Bernard. So you can only imagine the relief I felt when I heard the paper was no longer required. Don't get me wrong. I was sad to learn that my teacher passed away for she was passionate and cared about her students. But I was elated that I was no longer haunted by this paper.

All of my hard work paid off. In my senior year of high school, I had an "A" average, which qualified me to graduate with honors and made me eligible to apply to several colleges and universities. Only a few months and a walk down the aisle away from proving Charles and Bernard wrong, a trip to my high school guidance counselor fatally broke my spirits and crushed my self-image.

Picture a happy and overly excited Lashana with a big smile and full of energy entering a guidance counselor's office. The office was void of color, papers everywhere and had furniture that looked like it was passed down from when my mother attended the school. Despite the office's crappy décor, I was full of color, ready to talk about my future. My possibilities were endless.

But in less than five minutes, my smile quickly turned into a frown. After a weak handshake, we both sat down to talk about my college options. She didn't ask me any questions about my goals, career aspirations or plans for the future. It was if she was pressed for time, and having a conversation with me was not on her scheduled agenda. She spent two minutes reviewing my transcript, which indicated to me that she didn't even bother to prepare for our meeting. Her lack of preparation would have been less offensive if her first question to me wasn't, "Have you considered going to community college?"

My eyes popped out of my head; I couldn't believe this lady had the audacity to ask me this. What was in my transcript that would lead her to position community college as my only option? It was at this time the demon of self-hate whispered in my ear, "See, you didn't fool everyone. She knows you're not smart."

Somehow, I found the composure not to just walk out of her office, but also not to use my extensive vocabulary of four-letter words. Fortunately, I was able to manage a soft sarcastic, "No, I never considered community college."

She proceeded to take another blow to my self-confidence. She followed her offensive question with "You should consider community college. This may be your best and only chance of getting a degree. You can get an associate's degree and land a good job."

That was the last thing I heard because my head was swirling with four-letter responses that would have gotten me kicked out of her office and suspended from school. So instead of exacerbating the situation, I zoned out and prayed that the torture would be over soon. Just my luck, I was only worthy of ten minutes of her time, so I didn't have to endure her bullshit for too much longer.

After this meeting, the demon of self-hate was in rare form – saying things that made me doubt my decision to apply to universities. Anger was the only emotion I could muster without breaking down in tears in the school halls. Her words cut through my self-esteem like a knife. I didn't have the power to fight, so I allowed myself to succumb to the deprecating words of the demon of self-hate.

I was no longer able to dispute the words and opinion of others. I was defeated and didn't have the fight in me to persevere. I succumbed to the belief that I was a failure and was never going to be a success. They won!!!

My negative belief manifested itself in my efforts in applying to colleges. I put in a minimal amount of effort, because I didn't see the point in trying too hard since I wasn't going to get accepted anyway. What college would accept me – an average student with less than impressive SAT scores, no extra-curricular activities and no money? It was thoughts like this that made me believe I was never going to realize my dreams of being a successful accountant, climbing the corporate ladder in a big accountant firm. I thought to myself that it was stupid of me to believe that I was ever going to be anything more than a statistic. Silly me.

Her words continued to haunt me until I received my acceptance letter from one of the best state universities. It took everything I had not to go up to the school and smack the guidance counselor with my acceptance letter. Although I was able to dismiss her words from my thoughts, I was unable to remove the impact her words had on my confidence. Her words combined with my struggle to maintain good grades made me question my intelligence. Was I smart, or were my grades the result of a poor school system? The answer to this question haunted me in college and throughout my career.

CHAPTER 17

THE PATH TO HEALING: SELF-CONFIDENCE

Along this journey, I found myself staring at people who appeared to be confident – looking as if they had it all together. I'd question whether their outward appearance was a disguise to hide a shattered self-esteem, diminished self-worth or lack of self-confidence. Or was their confidence a product of years of love and nurturing – the outcome of what a person could become if they were told, "You can do and be anything you set your mind to"? I wondered what life would be like if I didn't live in fear of the demon of self-hate.

Of all my journeys, the journey to self-confidence was and is the most difficult. To this day, I continue to struggle with wavering confidence. Through the exercises my therapist assigned, and some very emotional conversations with myself in the mirror, I was finally able to love the reflection staring back at me. I learned to appreciate my conservative, chic, classy style of dress. And at some point, getting dressed was no longer a chore. It was fun. I would do my happy dance while looking in the mirror, say a few "I love you's" and strut my stuff out the door.

Despite my newly formed appreciation for my reflection in the mirror, I continue to question the value I bring to my personal and professional relationships. There are many days I find myself wondering why my girlfriends choose to have me around. What do I possibly contribute to their lives? And at work the same questions emerge, "Why do they keep me employed? If I went away for a month without telling anyone, would the impact of my absence be non-existent?"

So, you see my journey continues. But instead of allowing these negative thoughts to cripple me, I now refer back to everything I've learned along the way, using a combination of the exercises, support from my circle, and of course, a lot of help from God.

INSIGHTS I learned on my journey:

I. THE BATTLE IS WON ONE DAY AT A TIME. There aren't any quick fixes, pills or surgery to rebuild my self-esteem. Realizing this helped me respect my journey. No longer did I have false expectations of my healing process. I now celebrate my progress and appreciate my journey ahead.

II. CLOTHES DON'T MAKE THE PERSON. My clothes are just an outward expression of who I am. My clothes represent my personality, but DO NOT define me. So in order for me to become comfortable in my clothes, I had to become comfortable with who I was – with the woman God purposed me to be.

III. I MUST LOVE MYSELF UNCONDITIONALLY. Loving me meant having an unconditional compassion and appreciation for the woman I am today and the woman I will become. It's liking myself with or without clothes, makeup (even the little bit of lipstick I do wear), or a fancy hairdo – liking me in my birthday suit. Loving me also meant enjoying time alone to get to know and love on me, doing things I enjoy and scheduling "me time" regularly. I must exude the love that I desired from others. For in order to be loved, I MUST love myself first.

IV. MASKS CAN'T HIDE EVERYTHING. Masks can only hide my external pain. The pain I felt within could only be removed by getting the help I needed to find internal peace, joy and love.

EXERCISES I used on my journey:

I. MIRROR/MIRROR. Do you know how difficult it is to stand in the mirror unclothed for three minutes, saying nothing but positive words of affirmation and then spending another minute saying, "I love you"? The first couple of days were painful, but after a while it became easier.

II. GOOD-BAD AND RIGHT-WRONG NO LONGER EXISTS. Since many of my beliefs were based on the premise that others were right and I was wrong and other people were good and I was bad, my therapist asked me to change my mindset and remove these terms from my vocabulary. As I did as she suggested, outside of legal issues (of course), I began to think about things as just "being." Things were neither good nor bad, right nor wrong; things were just "is what it is." For example, if I thought about the way a person dressed (whether whole-some or super sexy), their opinions (wheth-er radical or conservative) or their actions (whether polite or rude) as just being a part of who they are without judgment, then I remove the notion that any one person is better than anyone else. Hence my saying, "I am who I am!"

III. THANK YOU FOR THE COMPLIMENT. As difficult as it may have been, I had to learn how to accept the compliments of others without dimming my light – downplaying my accomplishments or deflecting the attention on them as not to seem conceited. So when someone said, "You did a good job" or "You're beautiful," the only response I was allowed was, "thank you." This was very hard, for my normal response would have been, "Oh, it was nothing. You're doing a great job, too" or "You would be correct if my hair wasn't a mess or I didn't look like I haven't slept in days." Damn, it was so easy for me to hold on to the negative comments of others, but I couldn't just simply accept a compliment with a mere, "thank you".

THE END?

Do you truly know the people you interact with on a daily basis – friends, family and co-workers? You may share your hopes, dreams and fears and on occasion, your most intimate secrets with people, but does this mean they really know you?

Relationships are very complex and often include a certain level of comfort, trust and doubt. We feel *comfortable* with certain people in our circle and *trust* them with thoughts and feelings we hold sacred. However, the subconscious doubt we as people have makes it difficult for us to share EVERYTHING. Try to remember the last time you shared something with your best friend. Were there details – if even the most insignificant – that you decided to leave out? And how many of you have good friends that only know you as an adult and know nothing about your past – the time in your life that shaped you into the person you are today?

The need for relationships is an intrinsic part of being human, and rightfully so, God made us this way. We long for close, meaningful and loving relationships in which we share our life with another person through conversations, experiences and intimacy. After being in your life for a length of time or after an ongoing exchange of innermost thoughts and feelings, friends and family members are disillusioned into believing they somehow have obtained an "insider's guide" to knowing you. However, no matter how much you share with someone, you are only giving them enough to have a superficial glimpse of your "true self." Think about it. How can anyone know you when you're still getting know yourself?

At this point, many of you are asking, "What is she talking about? I've lived with myself for "X" number of years, and should know myself better than anyone." For some of you, this is true, and of those, I'm envious.

I'm not the same person I was in my teens – thank God. I have also evolved from that extremely shy, depressed, and lost person I was in my twenties. And when I turned thirty, I thought I was well on my way to understanding and loving the woman I was. To my surprise, as I wrote this book, I continued to transition into the woman God has purposed me to be. Every day is like attending the "school of Lashana." I learn a little more about myself each day. I believe that I'm at a point in my learning where I understand and appreciate my unique imperfections.

For so many years, I've tried to fit into whatever mold I thought people wanted me in, which made it difficult to really know who I was. A chameleon amongst my circle of family and friends – they only knew the person I allowed them to see. My low self-esteem tricked me into believing that the only way people would like me was if I acted like them, or in some cases emulated the person they wanted me to be. Around my family, I portrayed this no-nonsense, motivated, independent, young woman who was confident and knew exactly what the future had in store. Although on paper, this person seemed almost perfect, the reality was that this was far from the person I was at the time.

It is said that you should not dwell on the past, and in most cases I agree. However, in order to understand certain things, you must go back to the beginning. Therefore the first semester in the "school of Lashana," I suffered through several courses on my past (history 101 and 102). I purposely used the word *suffered* because the events and the memories that were uncovered were less like a pleasant trip down memory lane and more like a painful exploration into my psyche – uncovering demons and feelings I thought I'd buried forever.

To cope with my distorted self-image, I fueled my actions with the hurtful words of my mother, her friends, my grandfather, as well as my teachers. I became the person I thought my mother wanted me to be, thus completely losing myself in the process. And to make matters worse, I harbored the pain of their words, "You're never going to be more than a statistic. You're never going to be a success;" and "I love you, but I don't like you;" allowing these words to dictate my progress in life, my relationships with others, and my self-image.

Living with a diminished self-worth, I lost myself in my relationships with Sean, Mark and Steve – wanting them to be my everything. I had friends, but I wanted them to be my best friend – expecting them to be genuinely interested in all of my issues. I now know that this was very unrealistic. Men don't really like to discuss issues, like women. They like to solve problems and move on. I wanted them to be romantic – like on television. And when I didn't get the rose petals, bubble baths and cards, I felt unloved. I was so caught up in my own emotional mess that I couldn't see that romance is shown in many ways. It could be in the form of planning date nights, making sure the house is cleaned when I know he would rather watch the game, or taking care of me when I got sick.

After my relationship with Sean, I found the strength to protect myself from a physically abusive relationship and vowed to never date a man whose love is expressed through a fist or open hand.

Steve didn't use his fist or harsh words to render me powerless. His weapon of choice was mind games. His manipulative ways had me wanting to assume the characteristics of the many women in his life. I thought if I became his "every woman," he wouldn't have a need for anyone else and then he and I could be a couple. It was so bad that on vacations, I tried not to get too dark because I knew he liked light-skinned women. Like I said, this man had me MESSED up in the head. I'm so glad that I was able to wake up from the nightmare. When I woke up, I realized that I'm perfect (imperfect) just the way I am. He wasn't able to appreciate, nor did he deserve a woman of my caliber. One day, he'll wish he never treated me the way he did, but until then, I will enjoy life being the wonderful woman God purposed me to be.

As I mentioned, self-confidence continues to be an area in which I struggle. Even as I write the last few words of this book, the demon of self-hate is in my ear telling me, "No one is going to read this book, so you're just wasting your time. Don't expect to be on the bestseller's list."

In the past, these words would have crippled me and you would have never been given a chance to join me on this journey. Fortunately today, I complete this book for me, and I'm happy to know that this book will reach the one or two (or millions) of people it's supposed to.

Along my journey, I've made a couple of detours, experienced more accidents than I care to remember, and suffered a great deal of heartache and pain. In addition to therapy, I also used my love of movies and music to help me through the healing process. Movies helped me to escape. And depending on the movie, I was inspired and given a sense of hope. I'm not sure if you noticed, each chapter is the title of a movie. Music told my story through words and melodies. Sometimes, I felt as if the artists created and sang the songs just for me. As I wrote this book, several songs resonated with my story, and for your listening pleasure I included a playlist that kinds of tells my journey through song. Through the combination of therapy, movies, music, and God, I was able to restore my self-image, and begin the process of rebuilding my self-worth and self-confidence. If I had to summarize my journey, I probably would list the following steps:

UNDERSTAND IT – I had to discover when – including the people and events – that stripped me of my self-love so I could remove my "stinking thinking" and begin the journey to healing.

ACCEPT IT – I had to come to terms with the fact that I have insecurities and battle with low self-esteem. It's hard to fix something until you admit there is a problem.

RELEASE IT – Do whatever you need to do (write, draw or sing), in order to release the emotion, pain and hurt that you may feel due to your battle with low self-esteem.

CONQUER IT – Victory is won one day at a time.

My journey is far from over, but I believe by sharing my story with you that I'm on the road to victory. It's wonderful that I'm at peace, filled with joy and enjoying life. How did I get to this place, you ask? For me it was a long process, but hopefully now that we have taken this journey together, it won't take you that long. As I continue along my journey, I will take heed to what I have learned thus far. These are not in any order.

1. A person will do as much OR as little as I allow.
2. I will no longer allow myself to be someone's OPTION; I'm a QUEEN and deserve to be a PRIORITY.

3. I have power!
4. I don't have to stay in a relationship that's depleting, no matter who it is. Every relationship takes work to establish, develop, and maintain. Going forward, I will ask myself if a relationship is enhancing or depleting, and adjust accordingly.
5. Expectations that are unmet lead to stress. I have to be cognizant of the expectations I place on the people in my life and determine if my expectations are unrealistic (i.e. they should know how I'm feeling) or if my expectations are reasonable, and adjust accordingly.
6. I can't continue to call myself a QUEEN if I don't DEMAND to be treated as such.

Thank you for taking this journey with me. I hope our time together has/will make you victorious over the demon of self-hate. Through my journey, I hope you are now on your own journey to rebuilding/strengthening your self-love. I hope you, too, can wake up FLAWLESS!

THE PLAYLIST

PART I SELF-IMAGE
Hate on Me – Jill Scott
So Ambitious – Jay Z
Shake It Off – Taylor Swift
Pretty Hurts – Beyonce

PART II SELF-WORTH
What About – Janet Jackson
Take Him Back – Monica
Final Hour – Vivian Green
Walk Away - Christina Aguilera
I Used to Love Him – Lauren Hill
Sweet Misery – Amel Larrieux
Love Rain – Jill Scott
Loving You No More – Diddy-Dirty Money
Best Thing I Never Had – Beyonce

PART III SELF-CONFIDENCE
Work That – Mary J Blige
Please Don't Go – Boyz II Men
Pieces of Me - Ledisi
Unwritten – Natasha Bedingfield
Flawless – Beyonce